SKETCH FOR GREEN
UDO DAGENBACH

jovis

IMPRINT

Cover and drawings: Udo Dagenbach
Photographs: Udo Dagenbach, except from p. 131, 179, 187–189, 193

Idea: Udo Dagenbach
Concept and editing: Bettina Held
Translation and copy editing: Ray Malone, Christina Wahle
Design and setting: Ursula Steinheuer, Minkyung Choi
Lithography: DESIGNPRESS GMBH
Benzstraße 39, D 71272 Renningen, Germany

Printed in the European Union.

Bibliographic information published by the
Deutsche Nationalbibliothek.
The Deutsche Nationalbibliothek lists this publication
in the Deutsche Nationalbibliografie.
Detailed bibliographic data are available on the Internet
at http://dnb.d-nb.de.

jovis Verlag GmbH
Kurfürstenstraße 15/16
10785 Berlin

www.jovis.de

jovis books are available worldwide in select
bookstores. Please contact your nearest bookseller
or visit www.jovis.de for information concerning your
local distribution.

ISBN 978-3-86859-632-8

SKETCH FOR GREEN

UDO DAGENBACH

jovis

TABLE OF CONTENTS

*"Curiosity
is the currency of luck."*

Udo Dagenbach

FROM MY SKETCHBOOKS

Udo Dagenbach

Sketching is a very individual way to express your ideas.

It always shows your vision. If you look back on the drawings you have done over a long period, you recognize a kind of common thread that links all the designs and ideas.

In 2017, I decided to review all my sketches done from around 1974 until now and present a selection of them in a book.

It seems that the technical standard of digital drawing pencils has meanwhile reached such a high standard, that they will replace analog drawings very soon.

Therefore, I see my drawings as relics of a dying work method.

I always refused to draw with the mouse, as I regarded it as a very strange and unsatisfying instrument. The connection between hand and brain was not as it should be. For hundreds of thousands of years mankind relied on its ability to shape its environment with its hands—developing analog tools as extended hands—but still depending on a good hand-brain coordination. The mouse has always lacked this connection.

With the modern pencil tools we can return to the analog structure of our archaic abilities, and yet advance to the incredible new chances the digital world is providing for our creative work.

I have never regarded my drawings as an art in itself—my drawings are expressions of ideas I intend to realize somewhere in the landscape, or they show how I read landscape and transform it into a sketch.

For 40 years I have been working in the field of landscaping, and for 30 years I have been working with glaßer und dagenbach landscape architects in Berlin. As you can imagine, lots of ideas, projects, competitions have been done during this time. Many of them have not been realized or chosen to be awarded in a competition.
So they disappear unpublished, although many of them are worth being presented. In a regular project, process sketches are often only the first steps, which later are processed into renderings, animations developed with Photoshop.

The process of design is hardly ever completely documented. Nobody shows a false design path, which could have been interesting in another project.

It is a pity that this work is slowly disappearing from our daily planning processes.

I try to draw my ideas as precisely as necessary, so as to be able to use the drawings as a means of communicating with the people implementing the ideas. So they are not too complex, they are easy to understand and, wherever possible, self-explanatory.

They describe the art and try not to be the art. They show a way of finding a form.

Sketching is a universal and international language. It is an intercultural tool of communication. One of our first and most effective tools.

As a kid, I did a lot of drawing. The first big input I received was during a visit to the newly opened Centre Pompidou in Paris. It must have been in 1975.

The surrealists, and especially the work of Marcel Duchamp, impressed me a lot.
The cooperation with Prof. Makoto Fujiwara, a Japanese stone sculptor (1984–1987), and an internship in the landscape design studio of Ken Nakajima in Tokyo (1982–1983) pushed me towards a Japanese way of thinking in my design that is still alive today.

The drawings shown in this book are a selection, which document sculptural as well as landscape design works.
I never tried to separate those two elements, as I think design is always a hybrid way of thinking.

*“Drawing
is the art
of taking a line
for a walk.”*

Paul Klee

DRAWING WALK

Bettina Held

Let me take you on a walk through the collected drawings of the landscape architect and sculptor, Udo Dagenbach, which span over 43 years. As he writes in the introduction, for him drawings are the 'relics of a dying working method'. That sounds rather wistful, but, from the point of view of today's landscape architects, it is an absolutely realistic assessment: Dagenbach knows all about the virtually unlimited visualization possibilities of today's digital technology, which is continually improving—he uses and values them.
Neverthless, despite the conclusion that here is a chapter coming to an end, he has looked back with pleasure on all that he has done to date, and decided to bring these hand drawings together and publish them in this book *Sketch for Green.*

"Drawing means translating a thought into a visual form, a process in which head and hand are equally involved."[1]

Let me take you along the path, the way of thinking Dagenbach has followed, a graphic way of thinking, in which his means of finding and inventing form will become clear. Using some of his signature themes, this 'walk' will give you an overview of Dagenbach's world, the world of his drawings and his ideas. So that no one gets lost on the way, each of the works is identified by a corresponding catalog number and a page number.

Drawing

Design drawings are about realizing an idea on paper. In the drawer's head there is already a stimulus or a theme, or maybe even a conceptual idea. This is the first step to a work, or to the solution of a task, that will materialize in shape and form on paper, at first perhaps as a rough sketch.
To begin with, an attempt will be made to grasp and represent the essentials, omitting the inessential. From the initial sketch comes a preliminary design, then the final design; details will be specified, particulars worked out.
There may be a number of approaches or ideas, or variations on a theme (for example: *Stone Bench Design* (Cat. 5.

[1] Bernd Evers: *Der zeichnende Architekt* (The Drawing Architect). In: *Die Hand des Architekten. Zeichnungen aus Berliner Architektursammlungen* (The Hand of the Architect. Drawings from Berlin Architecture Collections). Ed. Bauakademie Berlin. Berlin. 2002. P. 103.

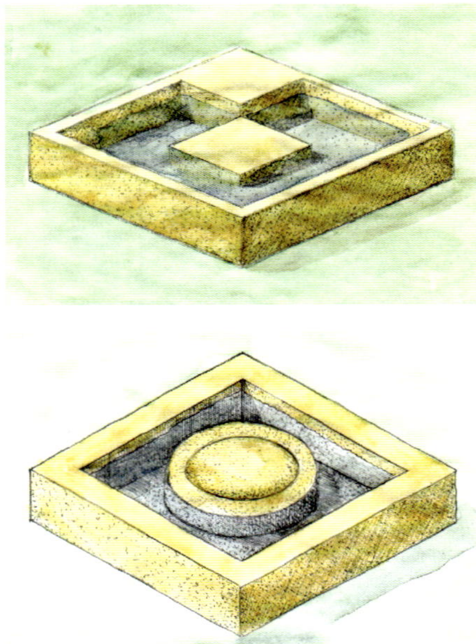

Birdbath Designs Cat. 3. Var. 2 and 4

Var. 1–8, p. 32–37); *Birdbath Designs* (Cat. 3. Var. 1–4, p. 28–31); and, perhaps, a desire to give the client several solutions to choose from.

Proportions and perspective, the visualization of three-dimensional space on a two-dimensional surface, the division of masses, the rendering of sculptural volumes, and the accentuation of bright and dark, light and shade: all stem not from a machine, but from the individual skill of the artist. Maybe, during the design process, the materials that could be used will be thought about: the type of stone, the plants, and so on. Maybe technical data and dimensions have already been specified, or indications as to implementation, or the ideal position in a given context. If the resulting drawing visualizes what the drawer had in mind—it is developed, resolved, and clarified in the process of drawing—the drawing will be signed off with the date and place of its creation, as well as the author's signature.

Sculpture and Landscape

In the beginning, Udo Dagenbach's inclinations wavered between sculpture and landscape architecture. Whilst working with the Japanese sculptor Makoto Fujiwara from 1984 to 1987, it became clear to him that sculpture alone was not enough: he became aware of how important, for an outdoor sculpture, the site and surroundings are! How decisive their placement, the carefully considered position, as well as the way they harmonize with other elements in gardens and parks are!

As a student of landscape architecture at the Technische Universität Berlin, Dagenbach acquired the ability to create such contextual relationships. The ideal combination of the two artistic approaches, sculpture and landscape design, represents the fundamental basis of Dagenbach's work.

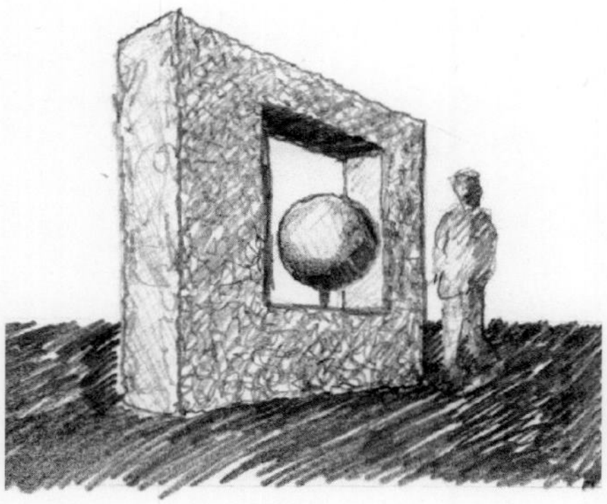

Plant Sculpture Cat. 15. Var. 4

Flying Stone Discus Cat. 27

Material and Surface

The organic and inorganic, plants and stone: these are the two basic materials of both landscape architects and sculptors. Whether in the overall plan or the individual aesthetic elements, Dagenbach brings the two into relationship in extraordinarily diverse ways. The art of sculpture and landscaping come together in the shaping of plants: in Ars topiaria. Hornbeam, privet, yew, box, hawthorn, and other woods are shaped into cubic gates, open cubes and discs, spheres, and ellipses, even into dynamic, torch-like objects, all captured in inspired designs (Cat. 15. Var. 1–4, 6–9, 11–13, p. 54–64).
In addition to that—and this is Dagenbach's very own idea—plants and stone are brought together to form a single object, usually in the shape of simple geometrical figures, such as cubes, spheres, and cones (Cat. 19–23, 26–27, p. 70–77 and 82–85). The plant, in being cut to shape, meets the stone, and conversely, the stone meets the plant, by, for instance, ridging its surface in order to bring it to life.
The viewer's eye is particularly drawn to the meeting point of the two different materials and surfaces: here, both in the sketches and the numerous realizations of such objects, the strength of the external form (Cat. 19, 21, 26, p. 70–71, 73, 82–83) may be even further brought to life by, as in *Flying Stone Discus*, adding a bronze core (Cat. 27, p. 85). However, even when the rigor of the organic-inorganic shape is maintained, and the form changed in terms of material (Cat. 20, 22, 23, p. 72, 74–77), what remains constant is the charm of these unusual compositions.

Transposing, Translating

A theme takes center stage: a school playground to be designed; or a park to be a reminder of a former historic site. The artist's fantasy blossoms. The pencil is 'drawn'.
With his two disciplines, sculpture and landscape architecture, Udo Dagenbach knows how to create ever new, always original transformations. To name just some examples: a redesigned school playground is furnished with two birdbaths conceived as instructive reliefs, one a plant cell (biology) and the other a Mandelbrot set (geometry) (Cat. 1. Var. 1 and 2, p. 24–25).
Public parks or gardens ought ideally be in locations that have a history: in Moabit, for example, it is the site of a former rail freight depot, where egg-shaped coal briquettes used to be loaded. Dagenbach takes this historical stimulus and translates it into a *Oval Briquette Wall* (Cat. 47, p. 140–141), which screens the park. Railway lines and tracks suggest the design of playground equipment (Cat. 48.1–4, p. 142–145); elsewhere they lead to the design of a sky-scraping railway track sculpture—unfortunately never to be real-

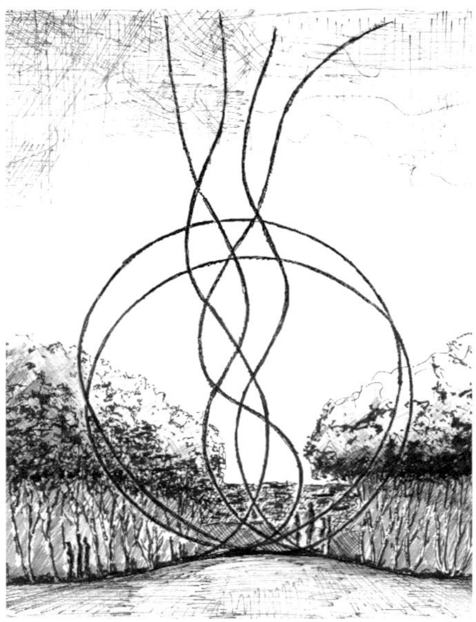

Railway Track Sculpture Cat. 28

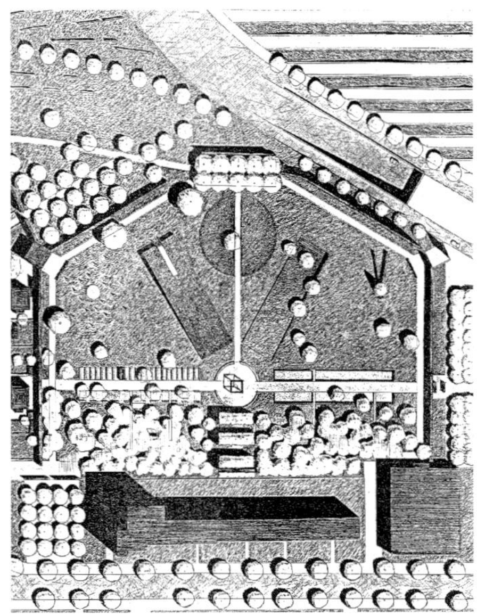

History Park Former Prison Moabit Cat. 41

ized. The *History Park Former Prison Moabit*, on the other hand, was showered with prizes (Cat. 41, p. 118–125): the austere formality of the garden as a whole, as well as the numerous details, are reminders of the former Prussian model prison, which stood on the site until the buildings were demolished in 1950. The early 19th century saw the innovation of single, instead of the then usual shared cells.
The list of such ingenious inventions and references could be continued: the Fabergé egg, for example, as a motif for a garden design in Russia. In the 19th century, the St. Petersburg goldsmith and jeweler Peter-Carl Fabergé based his valuable creations—creations which quickly aroused the enthusiasm and passion for collecting of the Czar's family and other well-to-do circles—on the Russian Orthodox tradition of exchanging Easter eggs. Dagenbach uses the Fabergé egg as the theme for a garden exhibited at a St. Petersburg garden show—an important field of activity for the artist's creative endeavors (Cat. 38, p. 112–113). The egg shape is translated into the clear language of a formal garden. The exterior of the expensive piece of jewelry, often set with diamonds, gemstones, and pearls, is translated into plants cut into shape, connected by charming spaces and pathways.

Dramaturgy between Heaven and Earth

"*This subtle relationship of line, of surface, and of rather horizontally oriented structures and verticals, and then to define them well, that is important. These are gardens, after all. And when it is well done, then it has drama, and something emerges from it, then it tells a story.*"[2]

Dagenbach's competence and experience in composing and combining diverse elements in parks and gardens—in particular the weighing of the directional forces of quieter horizontals against the more dynamic verticals—is demonstrated in his designs by their precise arrangement and appropriate setting. A column, or a tree, may become a particular design 'exclamation mark'. The *Stone Ball Sculpture* (Cat. 14, p. 52–53), in its first version, wittily connects both, in that Dagenbach places the column in the hollow trunk of a tree: again sculpture and gardening complement each other. On a semi-circular pedestal, a series of spheres of diminishing diameter, placed one on top of the other, stretch upwards into the sky. One is reminiscent of Constantin Brâncuși's Endless Column (realized in 1937), which is nearly 30 meters high. Dagenbach's design also fascinates because of the dynamic light-and-shade

[2] Mies van der Rohe Haus (ed.): *Udo Dagenbach. A Star for Mies*. Berlin, 2012. P. 39.

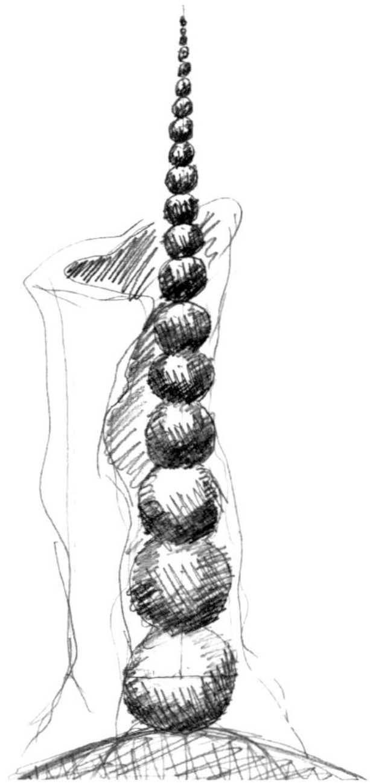

Stone Ball Sculpture Cat. 14

Endless Column Cat. 13

effect, achieved by the upward spiraling and underlined by the ever smaller spheres, creating the impression of great height: not only due to the perspective but to the fact that the round shapes actually disappear from view.

In contrast, the *Endless Column* (Cat. 13, p. 50–51) has a closed, cylindrical shape. A variety of types of stone with irregularly cut surfaces rise high into the sky, meant to symbolize the layered heritage of previous generations, to be passed on forever, generation after generation.

In 2014, Dagenbach designed kinetic sculptures in the form of plants—palms and strelitzia—for the Gorki Park in Moscow (Cat. 33.1 and 2, p. 94–95). Being almost nine meters high, their trunks, or pedestals, are made of crushed stone or cut cedar. The leaf sheaths and lamina of the multi-layered fan palm are made of steel and are flexible, as are the strelitzia flowers on the cedar pedestal. In order to fully realize their magical potential without the help of any mechanical device,

these vertical objects need the natural element of the wind. The sculptures, alas never realized, were conceived as landmarks in the center of the main access roads, near the orangery in Gorki Park.
An observation tower is also a vertical mark in the landscape, achieving its maximum impact when seen from a distance. Dagenbach designed three variants of such towers with different upward-spiraling, stepped ramps for the Schliersbergalm in the foothills of the Bavarian Alps in 2010 (Cat. 36.1–3, p. 102–103). In 2016, he designed a striking, expressionistic-looking vertical for the Astana Botanical Garden in Kazakhstan: a completely symmetrical, star-shaped network of pathways crowned at its center by a 26-meter high cathedral-like glass element whose steeply rising, shooting up points resemble a fairytale dream (Cat. 53, p. 152–153). The versatile creative imagination that such things tell of is exciting and fascinating.

Roots and Fertilizers

If you go looking for the artistic roots and fertilizers—in the sense of artistic fertilization—in Dagenbach's sculptural works, you come across Hans Arp (1886–1966) and Henry Moore (1898–1986). Henry Moore, in particular, believed sculpture belonged outside, that is, where their vitality and energy could

Torso Cat. 67

then flow freely. As with Hans Arp's work, Moore's is also characterized by organically curved forms. Three-dimensional, amorphously flowing bodies, reminiscent of natural shapes, seem to symbolize the essence and forces of nature: swelling volumes living according to their own laws. These influences, in connection with plant elements, can be seen quite early on, in 1974, in his drawing *Biomorph II* (Cat. 55.2, p. 158–159). Also *Torso* (Cat. 67, p. 180–181), from 1984, comes to life like a dynamically swelling, powerfully abstracted body. The opening of space, of 'breaking through', in which an empty space becomes an element in the design of an artwork, is apparent in *Inverse Wave* (Cat. 12, p. 48–49) from 2000, and, even more so, in the *Amorphous Aluminium Sculpture* (Cat. 35, p. 98–99).

The softly flowing shape frames the inner hollows, or recesses, while the towering double sculpture's outer contours correspond fascinatingly with the enclosed negative spaces. Such transparent art works enable the light and the surroundings to enter into dialogue with one another. The empty space is also an important design element in the strictly geometric works, particularly richly varied in the *Plant Sculptures* (Cat. 15. Var. 1–4, 6–9, p. 54–57, 58–61). Likewise, the *Gneissic Rock Houses* (Cat. 34. Var. 1, p. 96), where Dagenbach recalls the characteristic local stone traditionally used in houses in the southern Alps, surround a circular void: the design for a rural sculpture, still unrealized, shows the classical house shape, a cube with a pitched roof, made from traditional gneiss, framing a wide, tunnel-like opening, stretching from front to back.

The Japanese artist Isamu Noguchi (1904–1988) was a major influence on Dagenbach's connecting of sculpture and landscape architecture. Noguchi's artistic achievement was transgressive, in both its combining of Eastern and Western traditions and of diverse artistic genres: he melded artistic disciplines and influences from Japan with those of the Western world to create new artistic spaces, whether public squares, parks and gardens, or stage sets, such as those for Martha Graham, the American dancer and choreographer. Noguchi began as a sculptor. In the late 1920's, he worked as an choreographer at Constantin Brâncuși's (1876–1957) studio in Paris. With his rigorous simplification of form, its re-

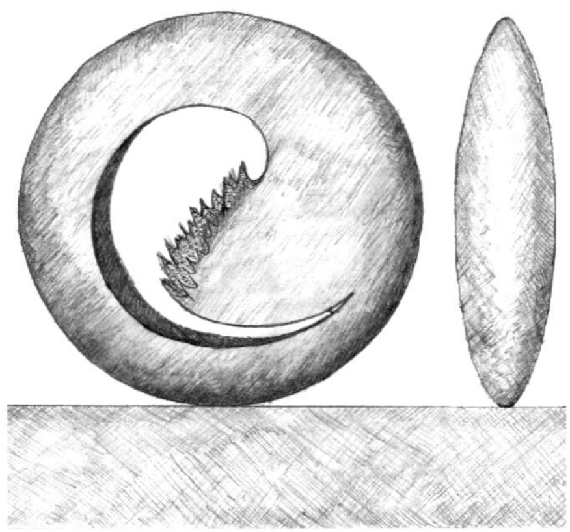

Inverse Wave Cat. 12

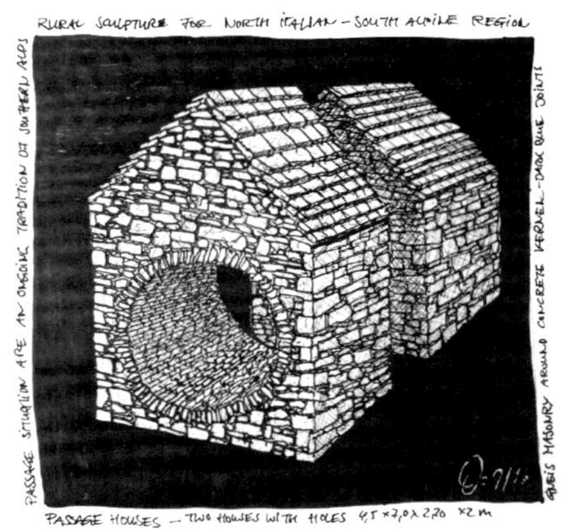

Gneissic Rock Houses Cat 34.1

duction to basic, elementary shapes, Brâncuși revolutionized sculpture, the power of the condensed, simple shapes paving the way for abstract minimalism. Noguchi adopted this approach, first as a sculptor, and then, from the 1930's, in extending the concept of sculpture, carrying it over—way in advance of the emergence of land art in the late 1960's—to the layout of squares, parks and gardens. Noguchi treated landscape as a material to be shaped and formed, as reduced and considered as his sculpture: clear, simple, timeless beautiful, artistically designed open spaces, in which the subtle synthesis of contemporary and sculptural concepts harmonizes with traditional Japanese garden design, where earth, stone, and trees interact. Noguchi's sculpture gardens offer the visitor a total work of art, to be sensed, experienced, and enjoyed, whether walking through them or quietly contemplating. Their example is tangible in Dagenbach's finely balanced garden designs, for instance, the plans for a *Private Garden* in Berlin (Cat. 51, p. 150), or one in Georgia (Cat. 50, p. 148–149). Natural/organic and geometric/rational shapes collide in the designs for a *Mathematical Private Garden* (Cat. 43, p. 128–129), and the four, particularly striking, adjacent *G'Mies Beds* which he realized in the garden of the Mies van der Rohe Haus in 2006 (Cat. 45, p. 136–137).

For Dagenbach, there is a further, third layer—the first being the relationship

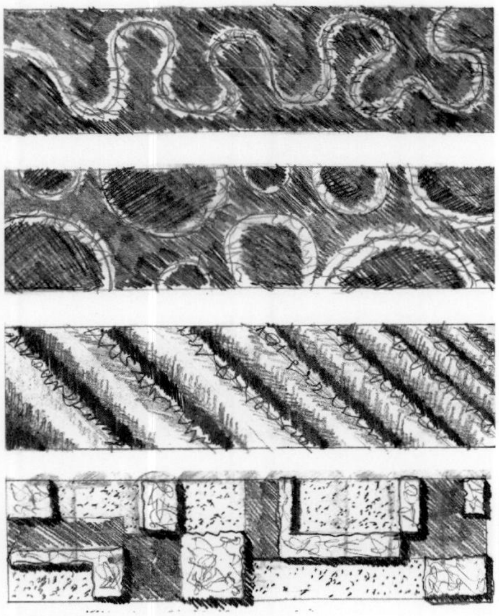

G'Mies Beds Cat. 45

between sculpture and landscape architecture, the second the relationship of the West to predominantly Japanese influences—when it comes to thematizing the history of a site in terms of both landscape and sculptural architecture (e. g. the *History Park Former Prison Moabit*, Cat. 41, p. 118–125; and the *Former Cattle Auction Hall* competition in Weimar, for a memorial with park for deported and murdered Thuringian Jews (Cat. 37, p. 104–111). The path leading to such a complex struc-ture takes the draughtsman through numerous stages—to do with the overall contexts, the individual parts, down to the details—to an outcome that, like a DNA, contains all of Dagenbach's concentrated expertise and experience.

In Conclusion

This book gives an overview of the diversity, the wealth of invention, and fantasy of a prolific graphic output, product of a masterful drawing technique, practized and perfected over many years: in the main a matter of gardens, parks, and their individual elements—the head and hand of the draughtsman engaged with the vitality of nature.
The technique of 'drawing', once purely manual, is being increasingly supplemented by digital aids. A great deal becomes easier and faster to realize: if you think, for example, of functions such as the automatic filling and coloring of areas, or working on several layers, or the enormous choice of pens and brushes, etc., or lastly, the speed of editing and sharing. That makes the professional's work much easier, without essentially influencing the generation of ideas or the style of visual expression in the process of drawing.

This book presents the output of the analog draughtsman Dagenbach's up to the present. It gives us reason to hope that many more ideas, both big and small, will find expression, whether on paper or on the screen.

SCULPTURES + IDEAS IN STONE

1.A
Realized Birdbath
Plant Cell
1991

Ideas in Stone

1.B
Realized Birdbath
Mandelbrot Set
1991

1. Var. 1 and 2
Birdbaths
Plant Cell and
Mandelbrot Set
1991

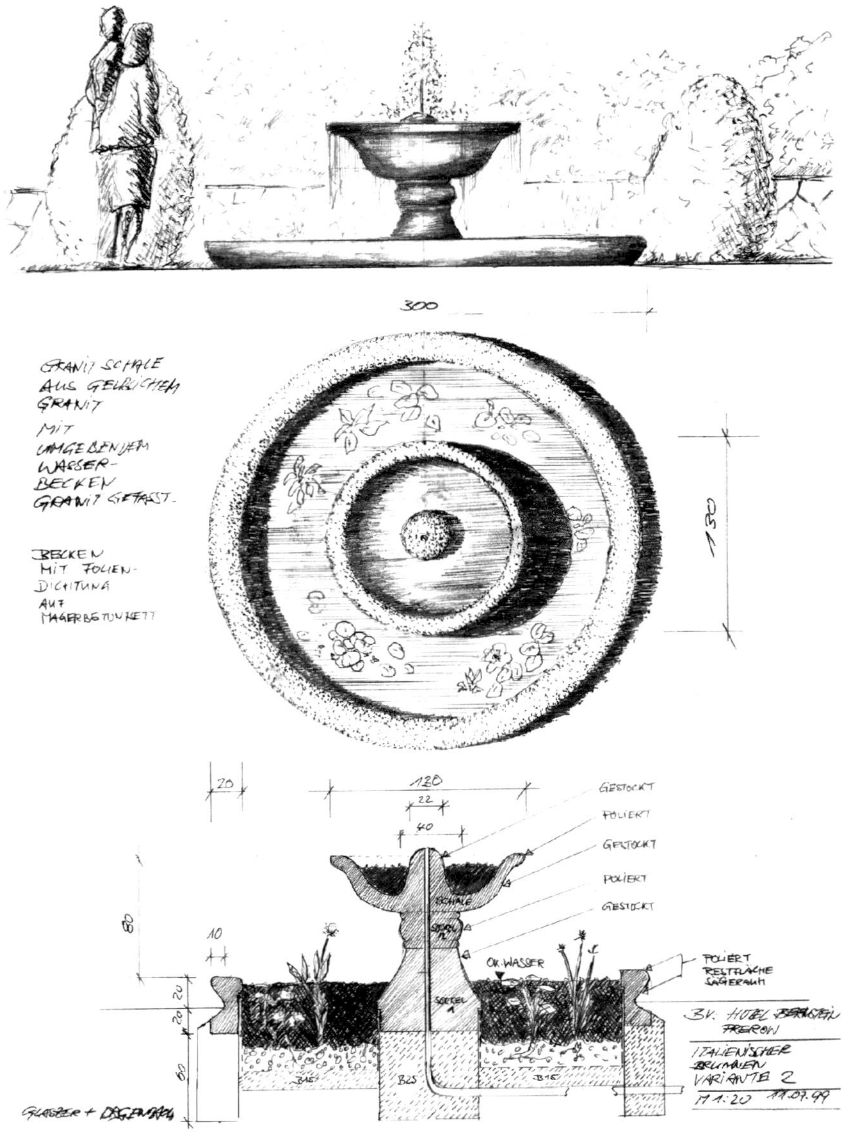

2. Var. 2
Italian Fountain
1999

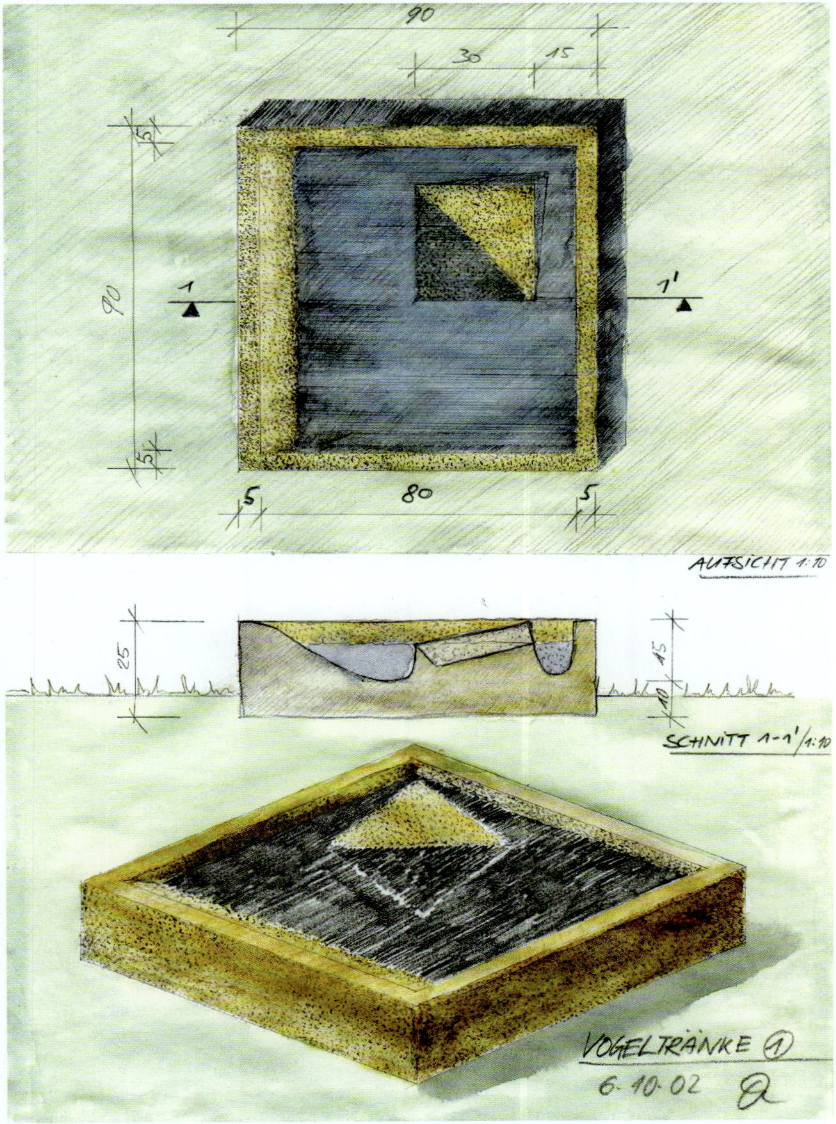

3. Var. 1
Birdbath Design
2002

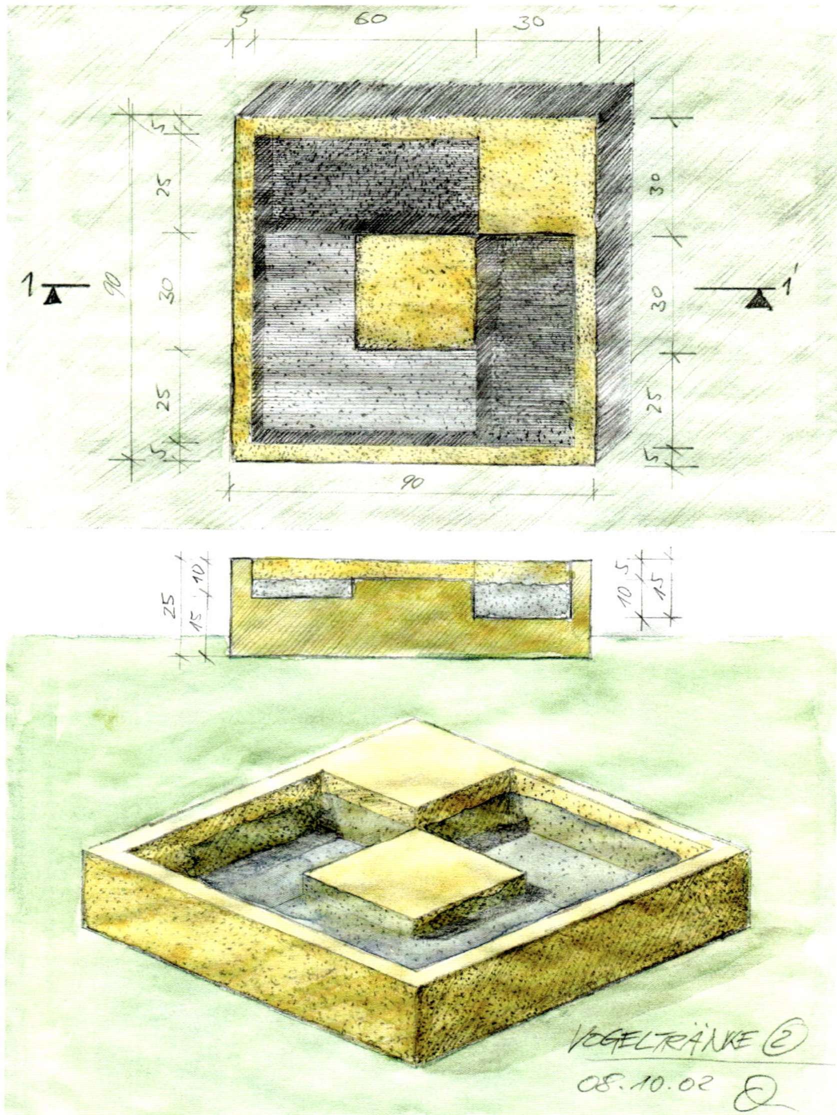

3. Var. 2
Birdbath Design
2002

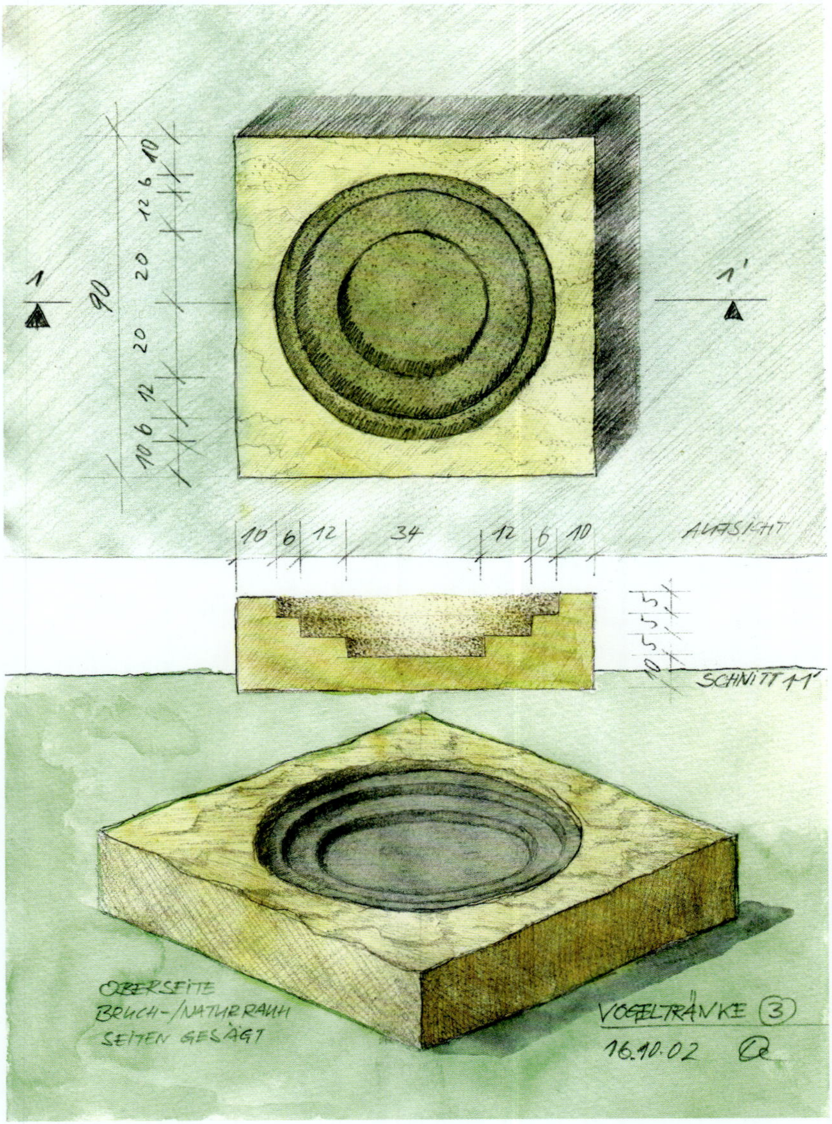

3. Var. 3
Birdbath Design
2002

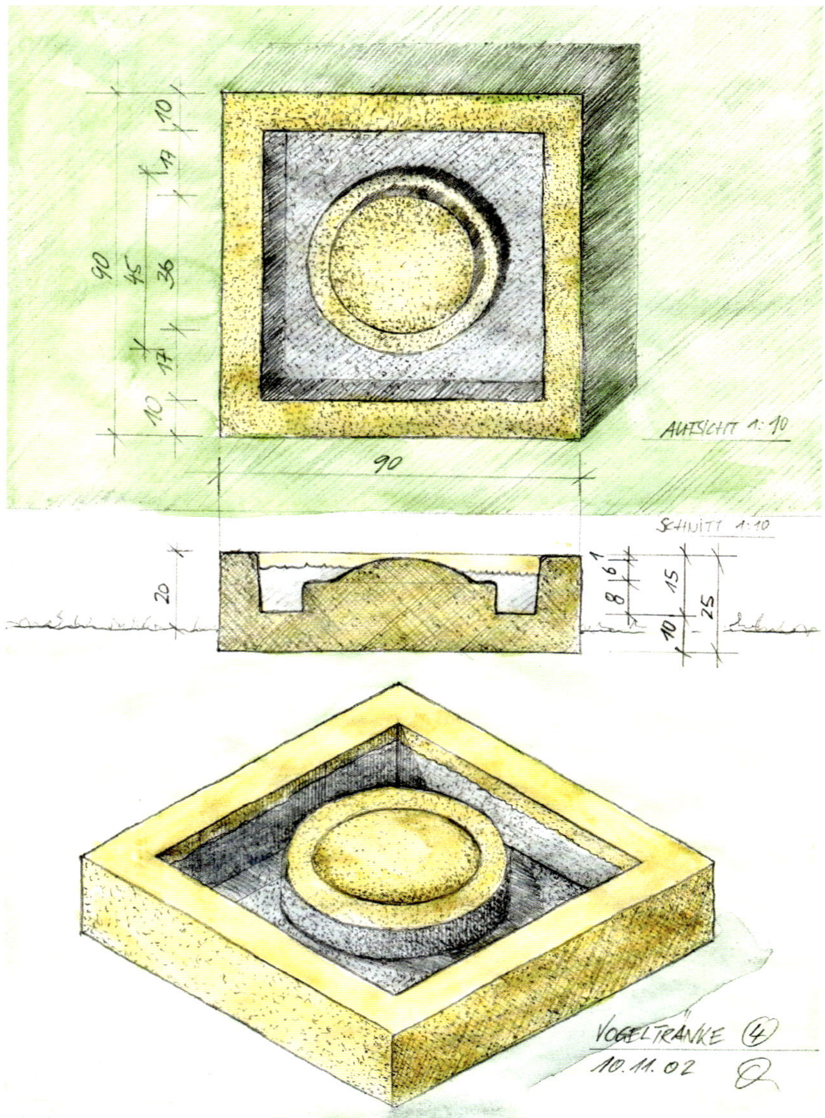

3. Var. 4
Birdbath Design
2002

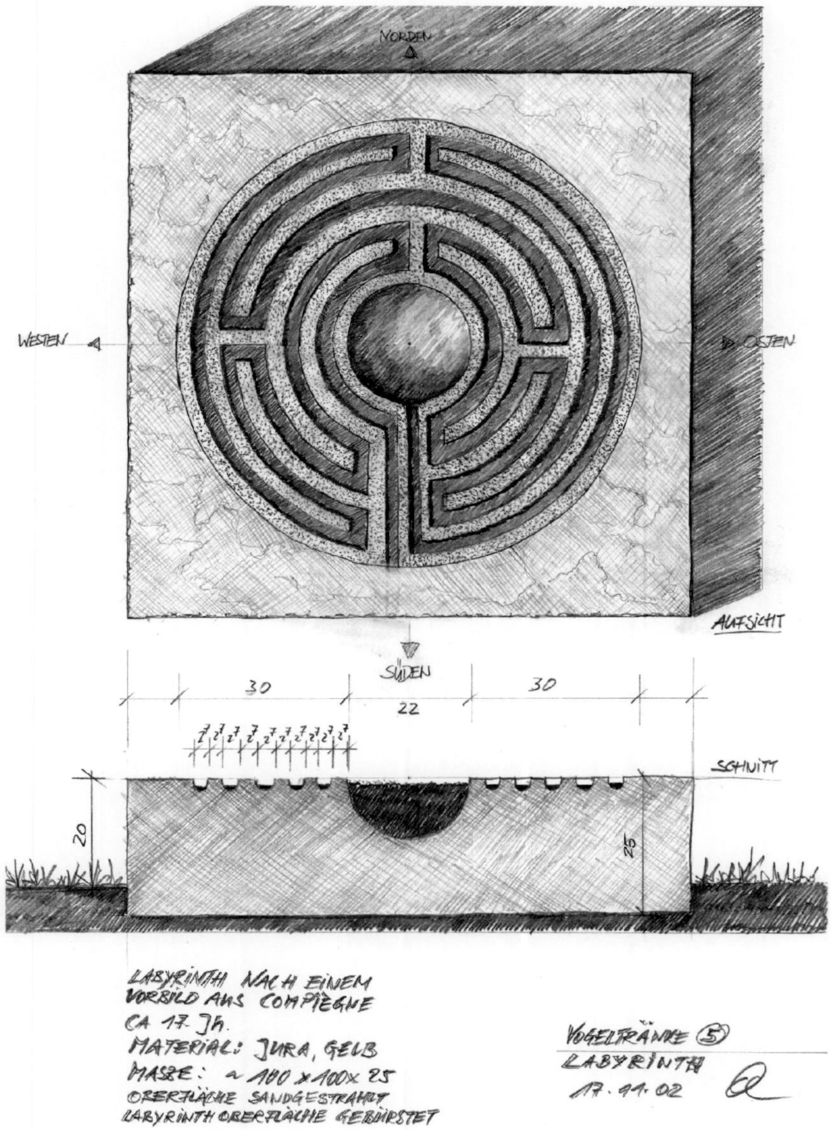

4
Birdbath *Labyrinth*
A later version
of the previous series
2002

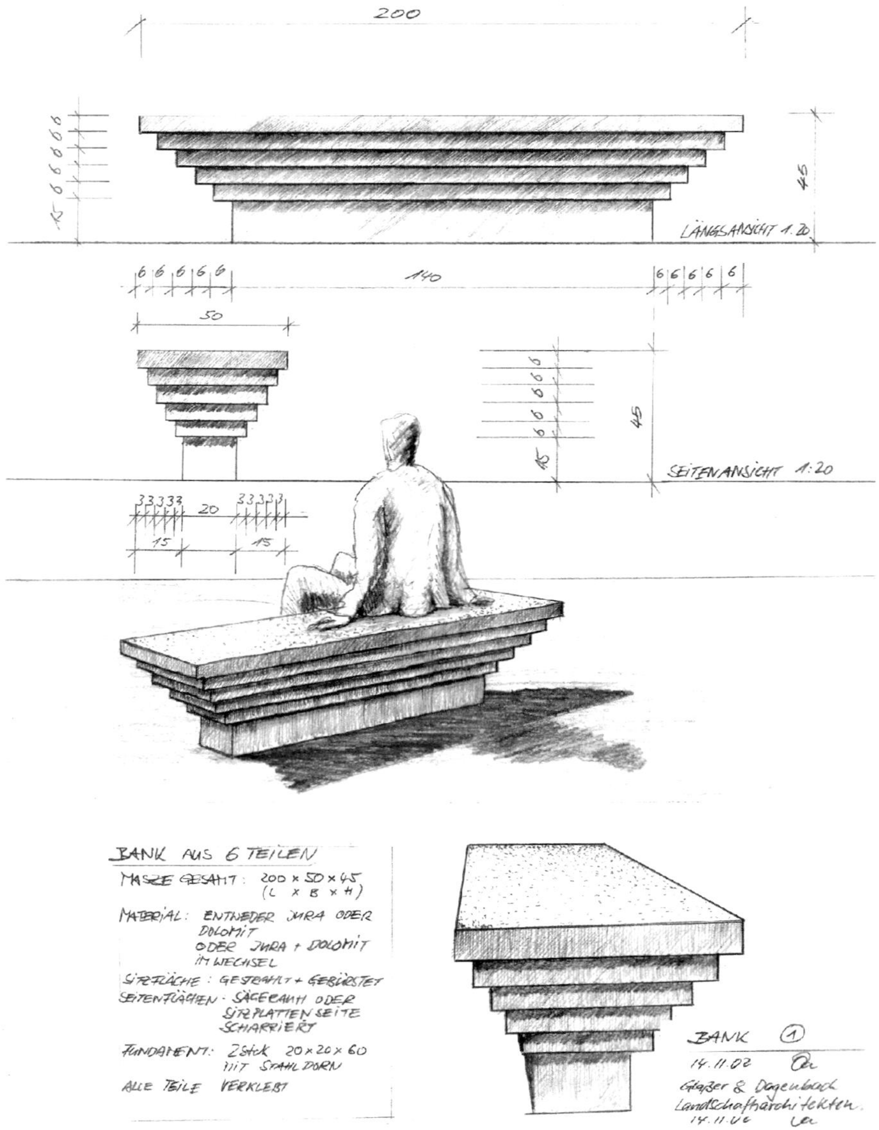

5. Var. 1
Stone Bench Design
2002

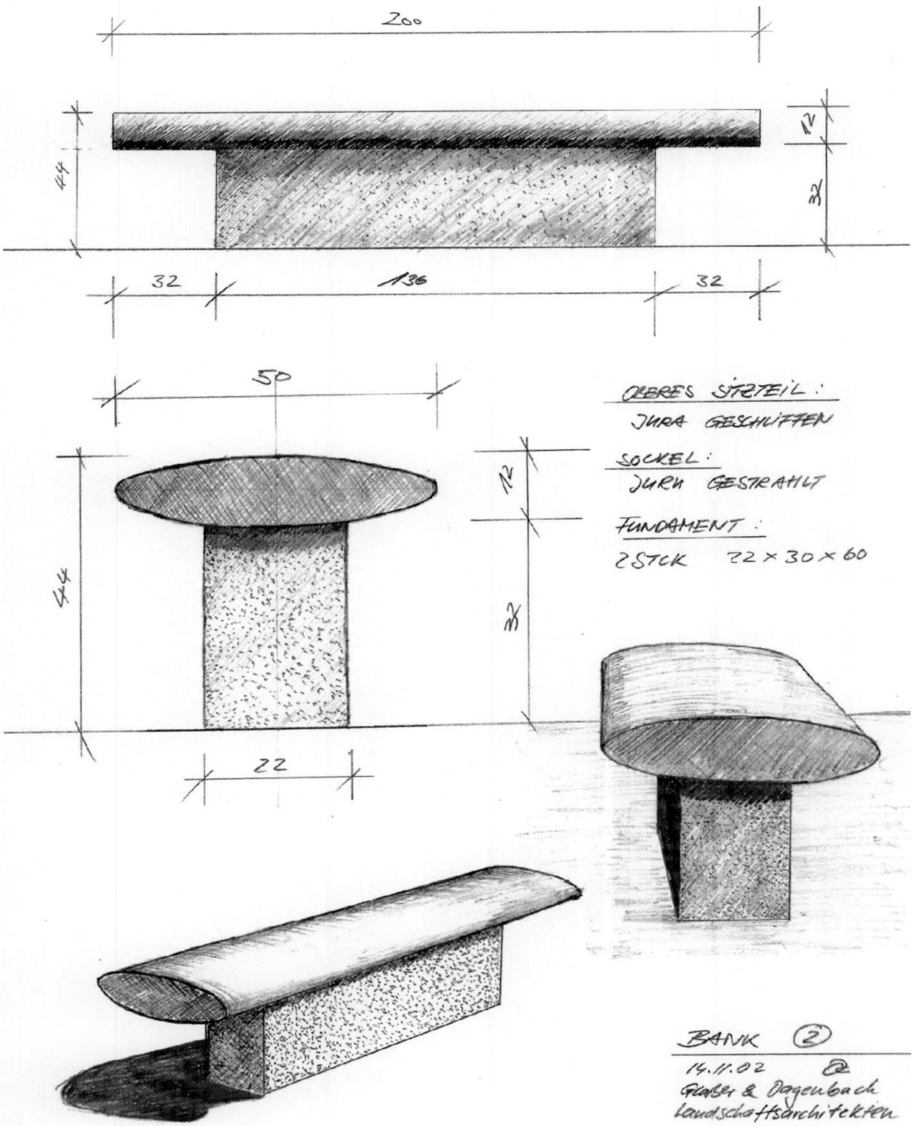

5. Var. 2
Stone Bench Design
2002

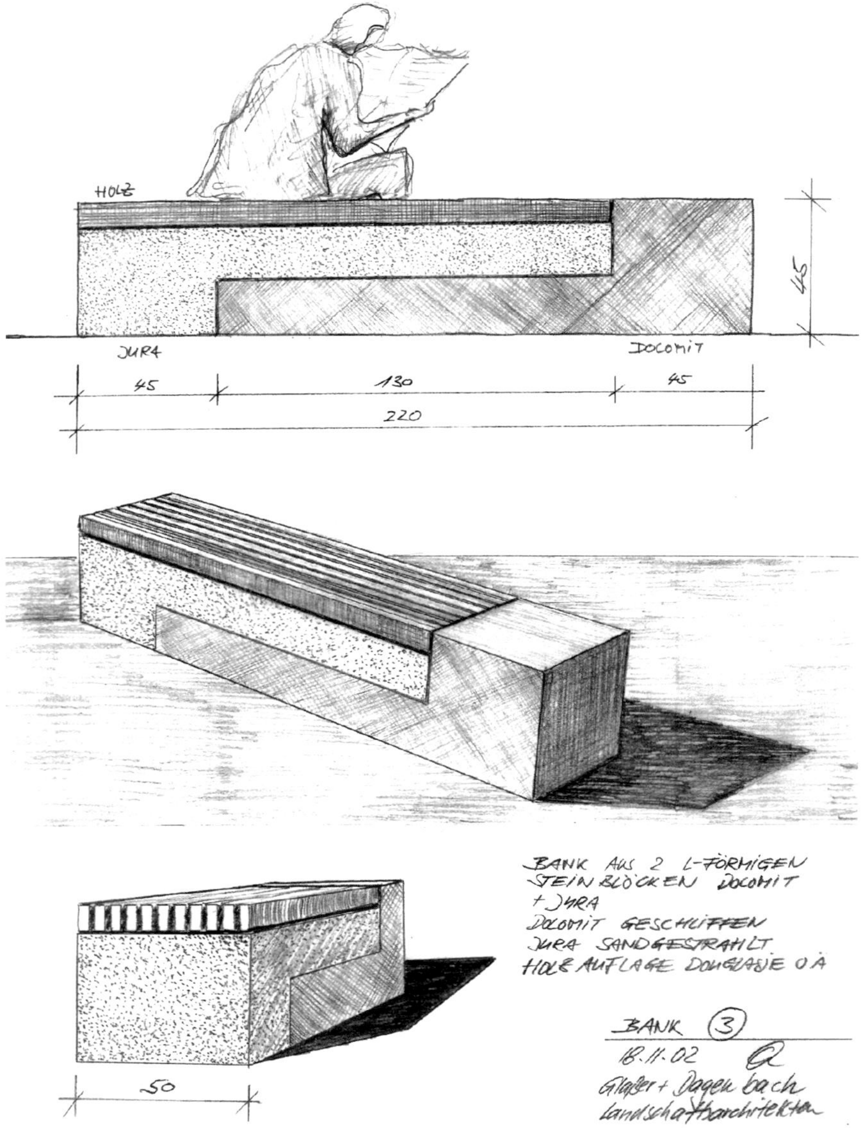

5. Var. 3
Stone Bench Design
2002

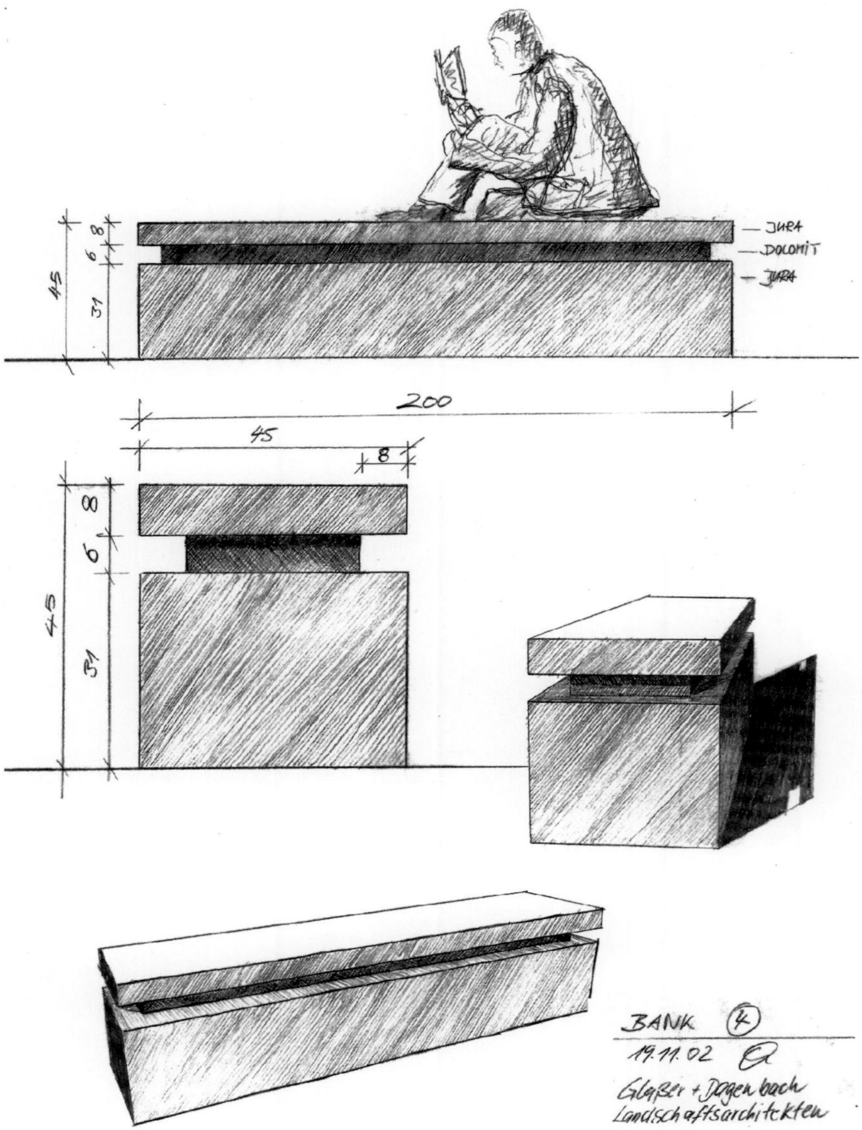

5. Var. 4
Stone Bench Design
2002

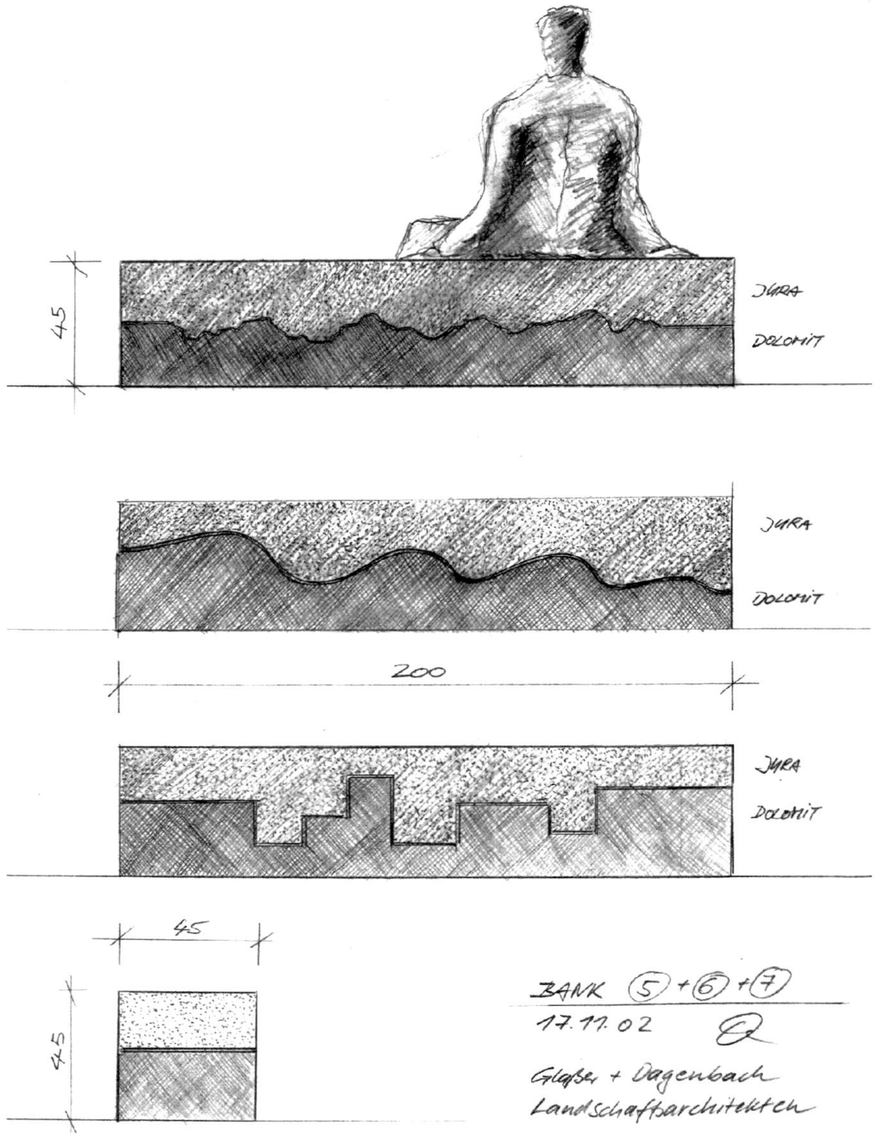

5. Var. 5–7
Stone Bench Design
2002

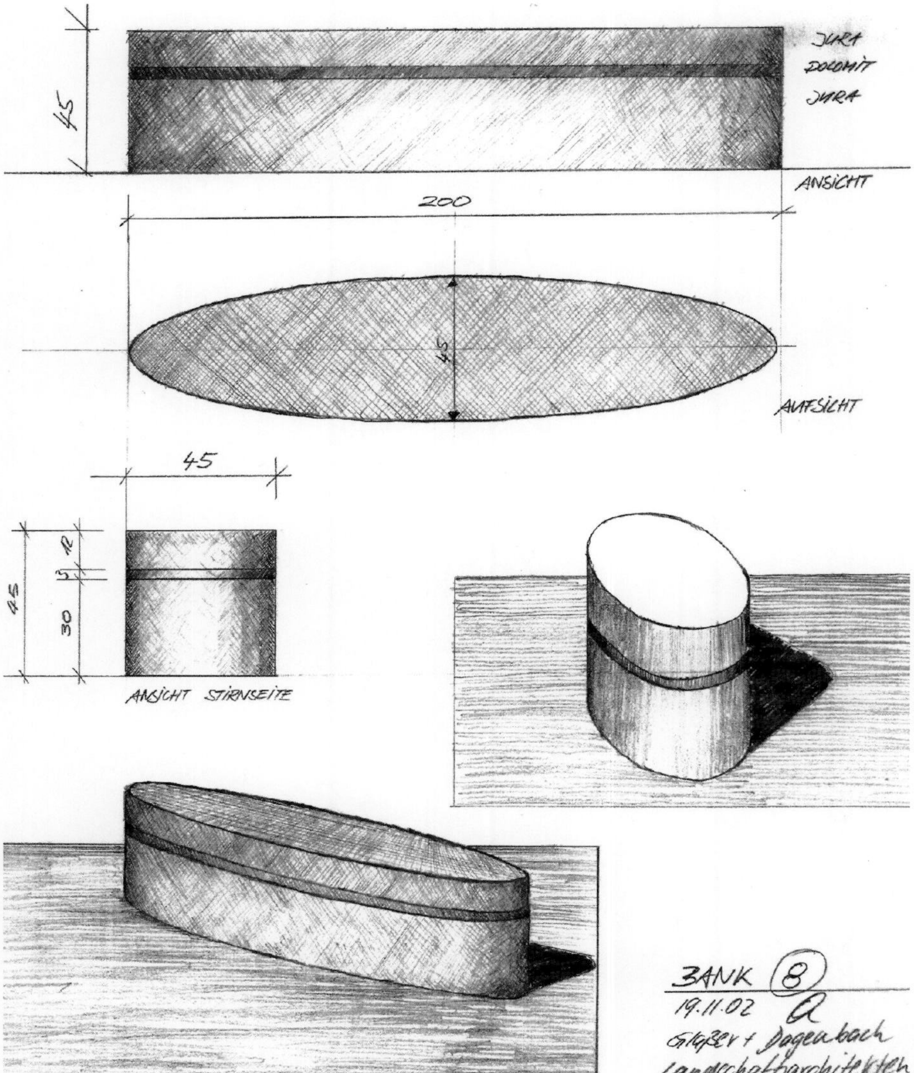

5. Var. 8
Stone Bench Design
2002

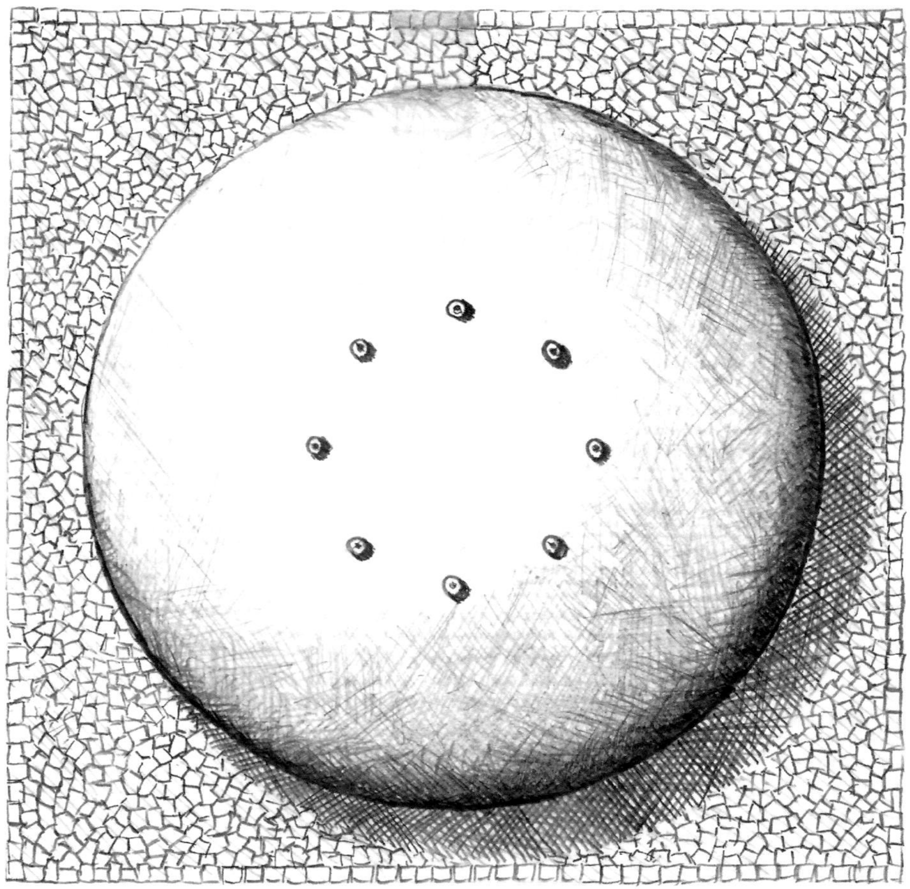

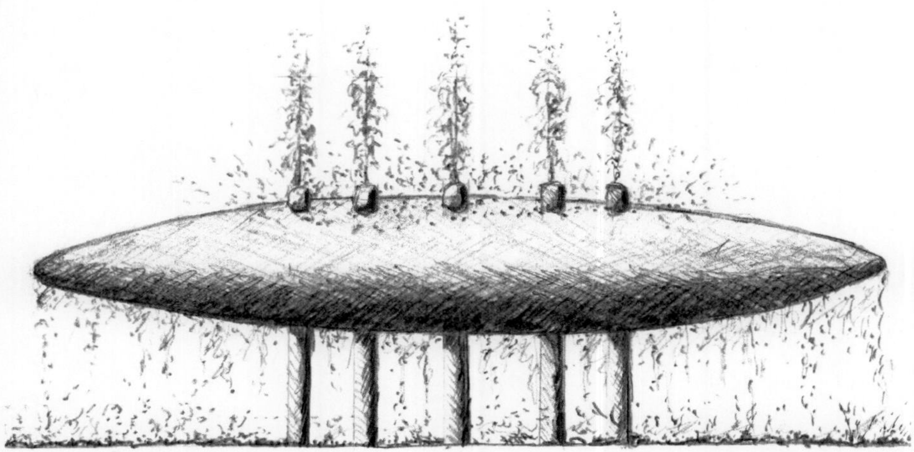

6
Lens Fountain
2003

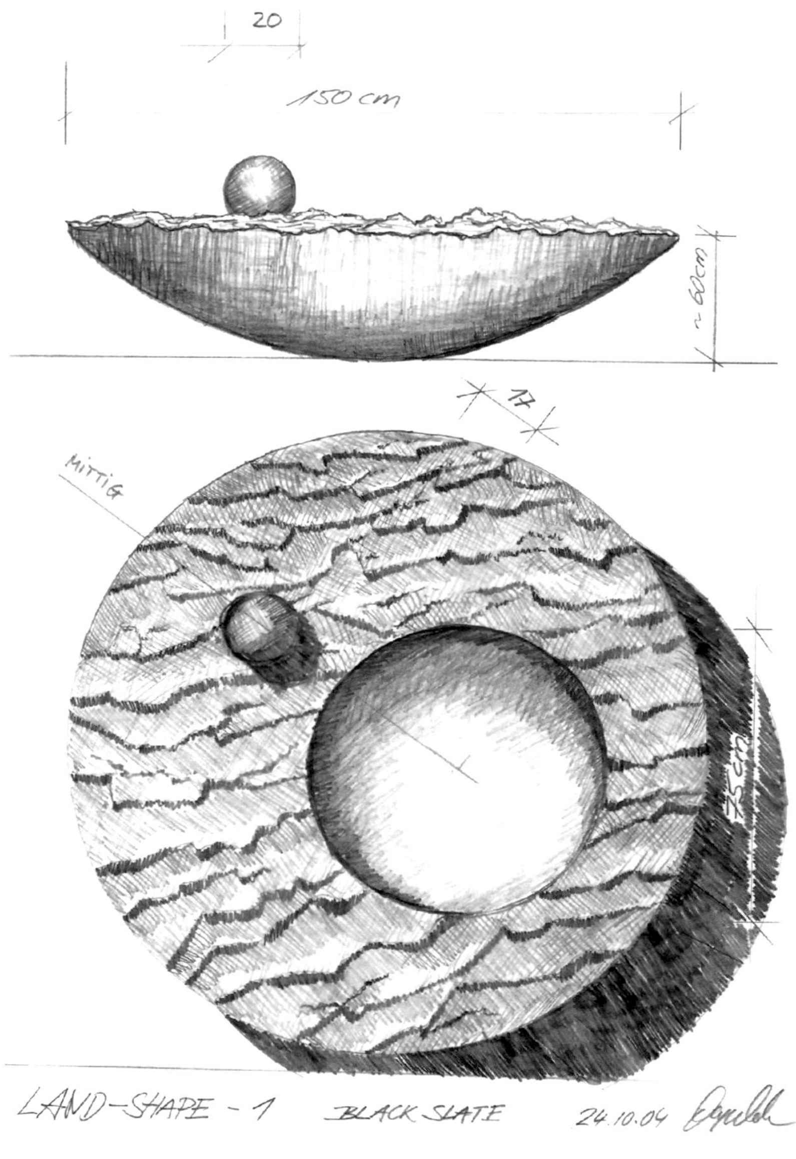

7
Land-Shape-1
black slate
2004

8. Var. 1 and 2
Cut Stone Sculpture
2006

Ideas in Stone

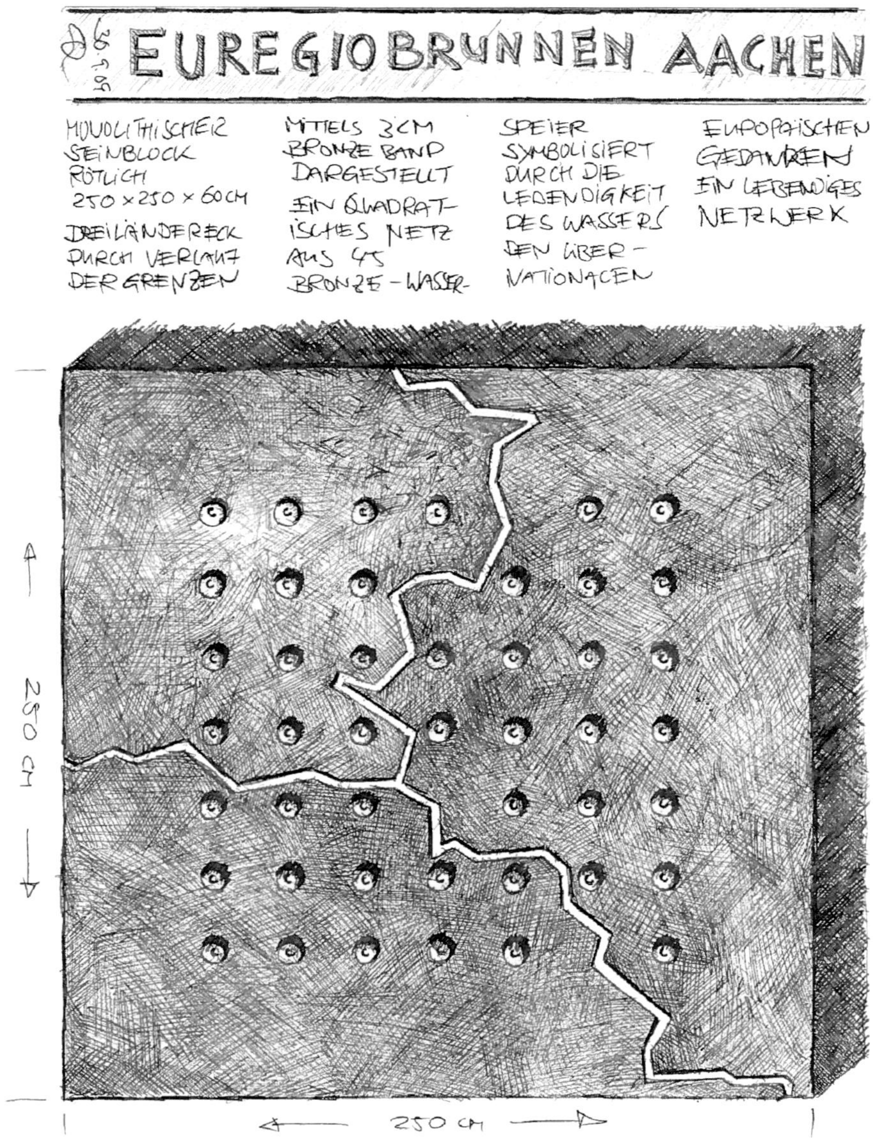

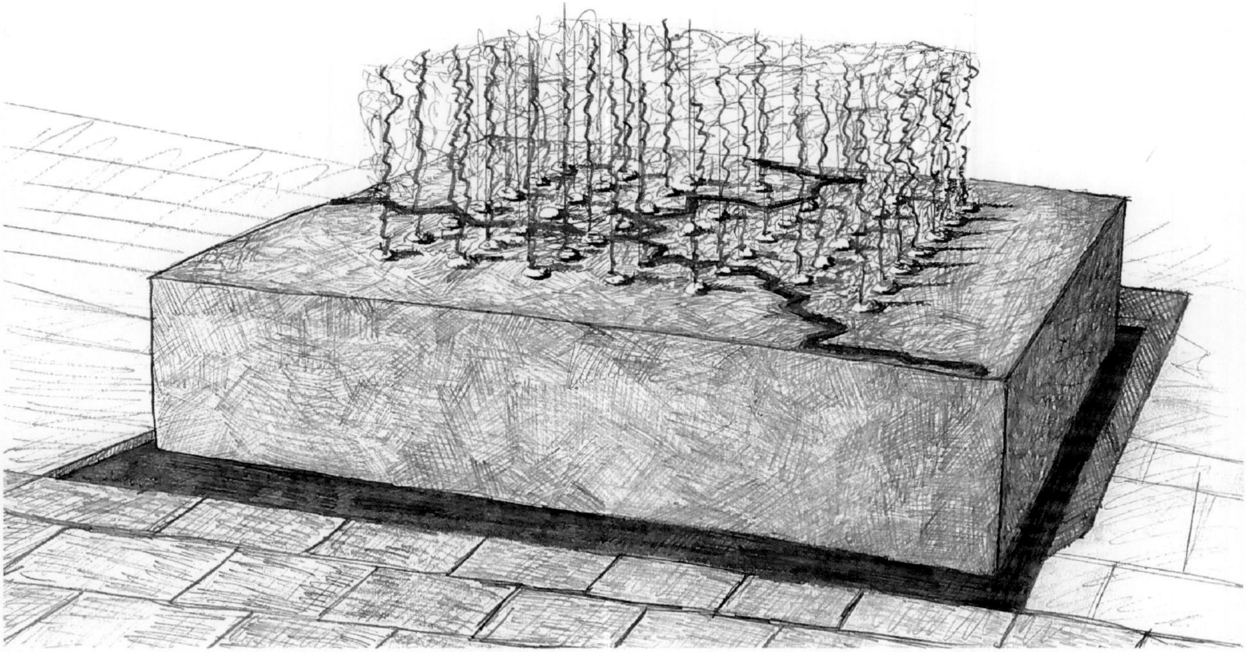

9.1–2
Three-Country Fountain
Euregiobrunnen
2009

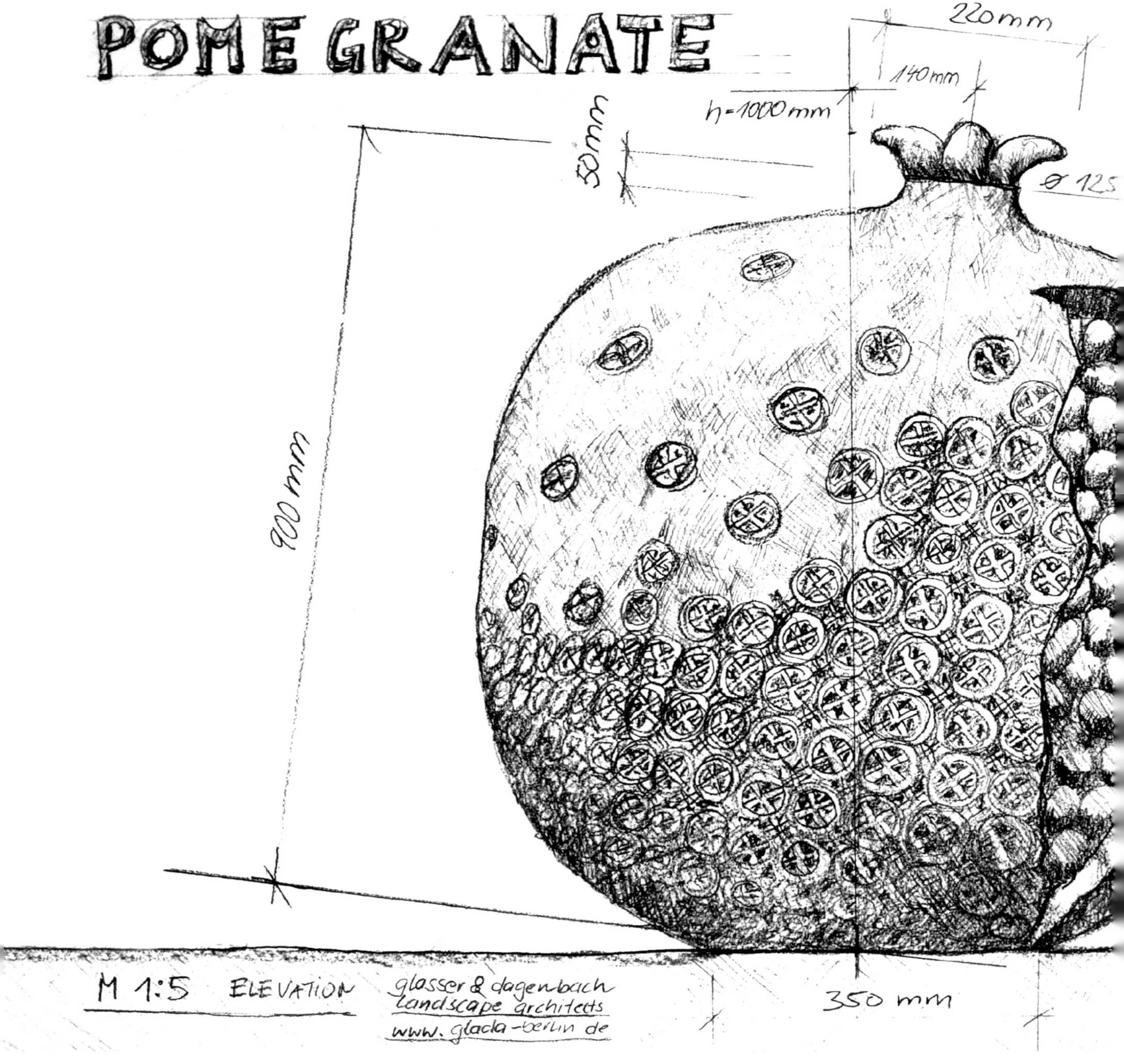

POMEGRANATE
220mm
140mm
h=1000mm
50mm
ø 125
900 mm
M 1:5 ELEVATION
glasser & dagenbach
landscape architects
www.glada-berlin.de
350 mm

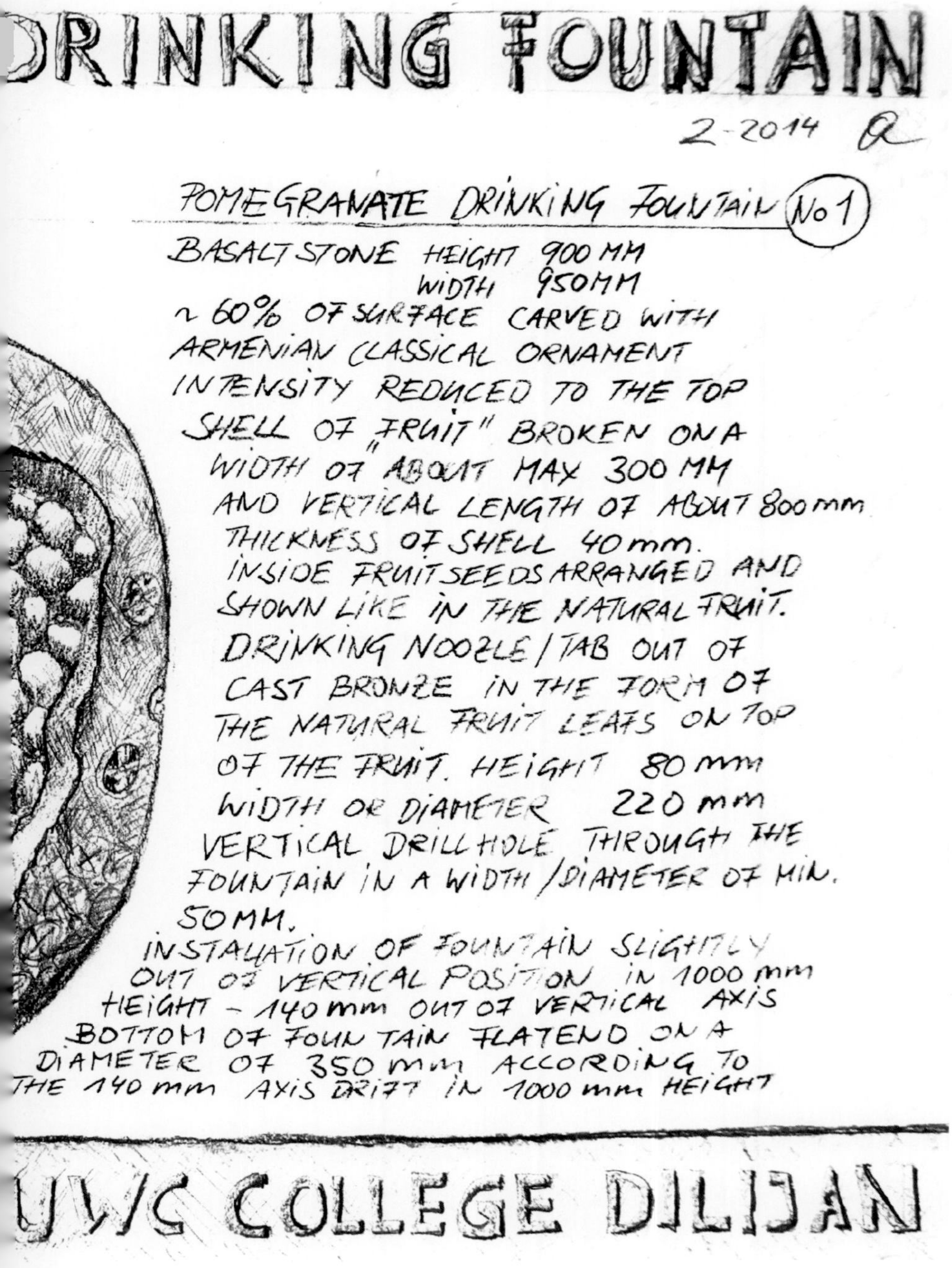

10
Drinking Fountain
in the Shape
of a Pomegranate
2014

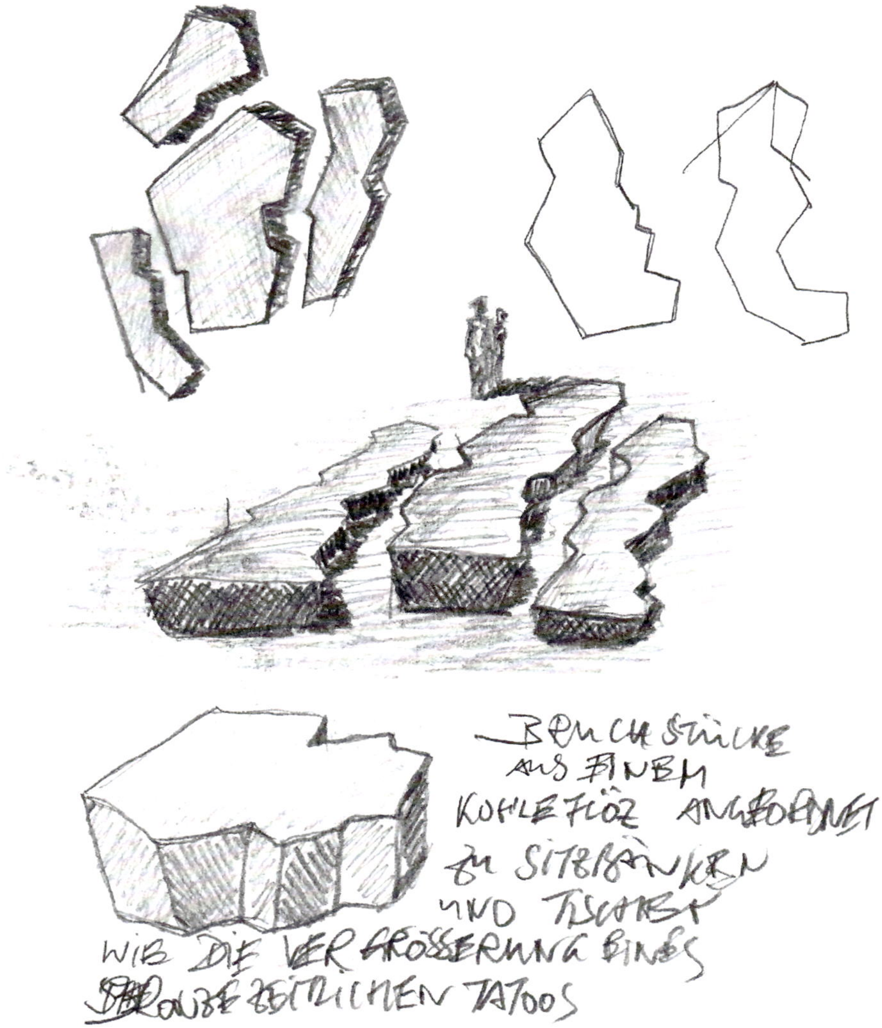

11
Volcanic Benches
and Table
2017

Ideas in Stone

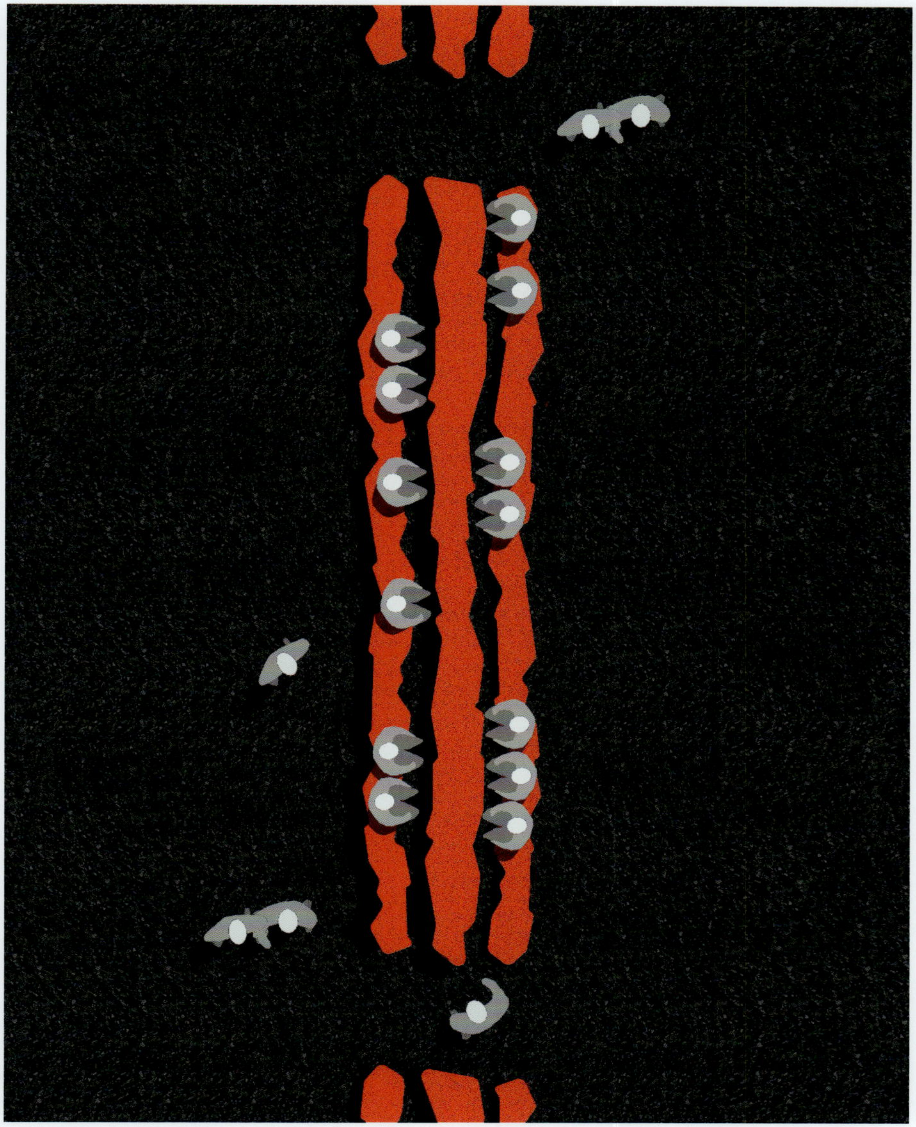

11.A and B
Rendering:
top and diagonal view

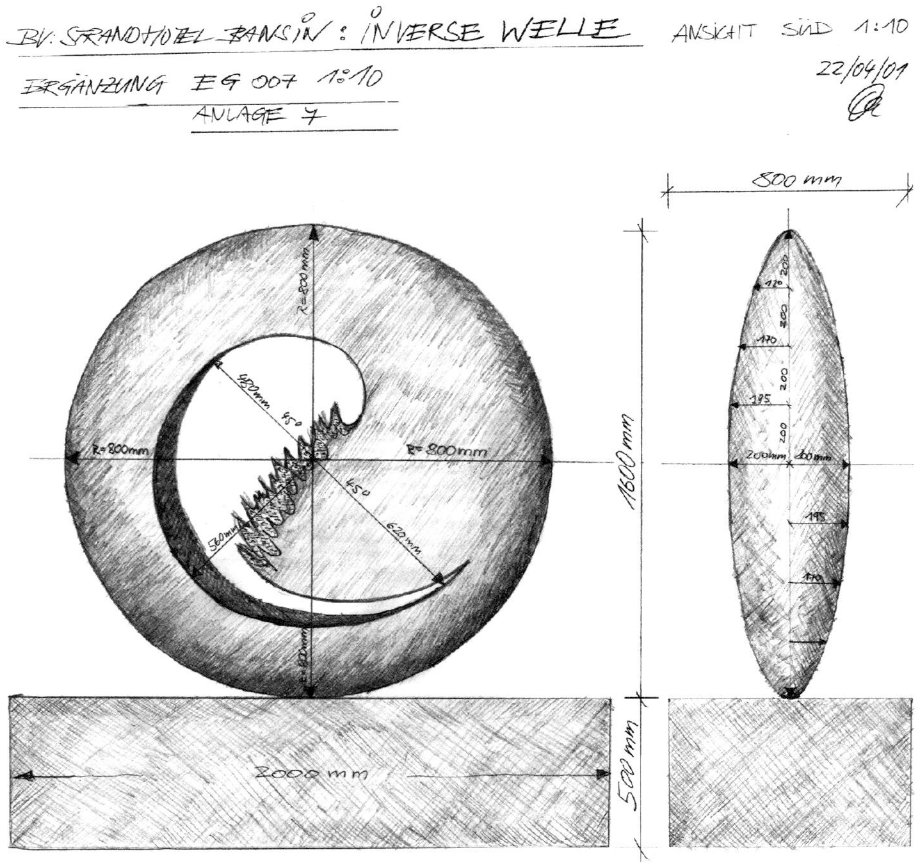

12
Inverse Wave
2001

12.A and B
Photographs of the realized wave in stone (2002) and in bronze (2008)

13
Endless Column
2002–2004

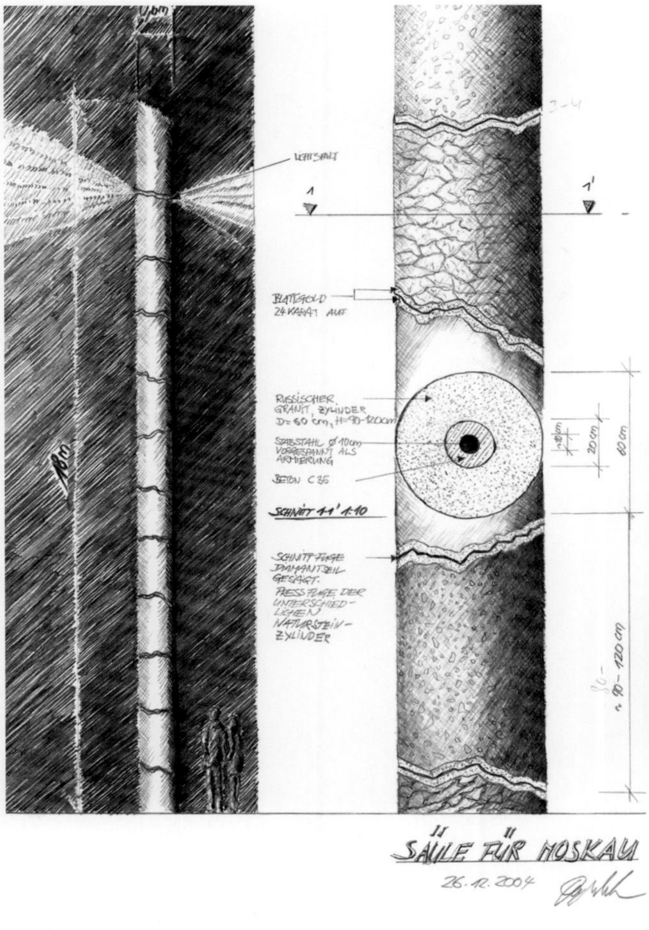
LICHTSPALT
1
1'
BLATTGOLD
24 KARAT AUF
RUSSISCHER
GRANIT, ZYLINDER
D=60 cm, H=90-120cm
STABSTAHL Ø 10cm
VORGESPANNT ALS
ARMIERUNG
BETON C 35
SCHNITT 1-1' 1:10
SCHNITT-FUGE
DIAMANTSEIL
GESÄGT.
PRESSFUGE DER
UNTERSCHIED-
LICHEN
NATURSTEIN-
ZYLINDER
20 cm
60 cm
~ 90 - 120 cm
SÄULE FÜR MOSKAU
26.12.2004

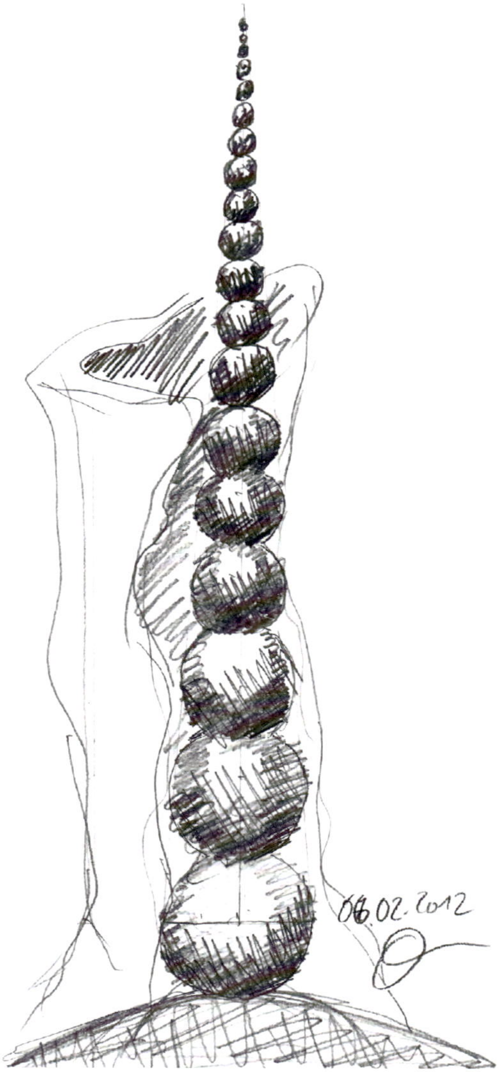

14
Stone Ball Sculpture
2012

Stone Sculptures

14.A
Rendering of the Stone Ball Sculpture

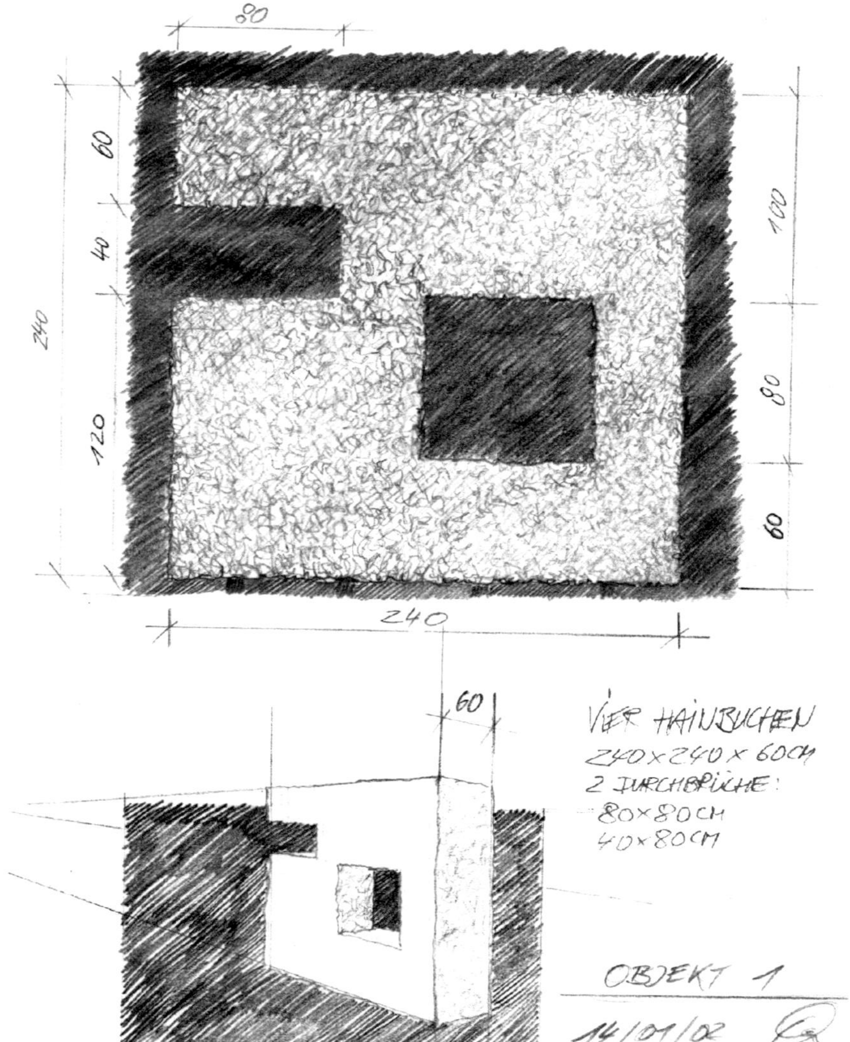

15. Var. 1
Plant Sculpture
2002

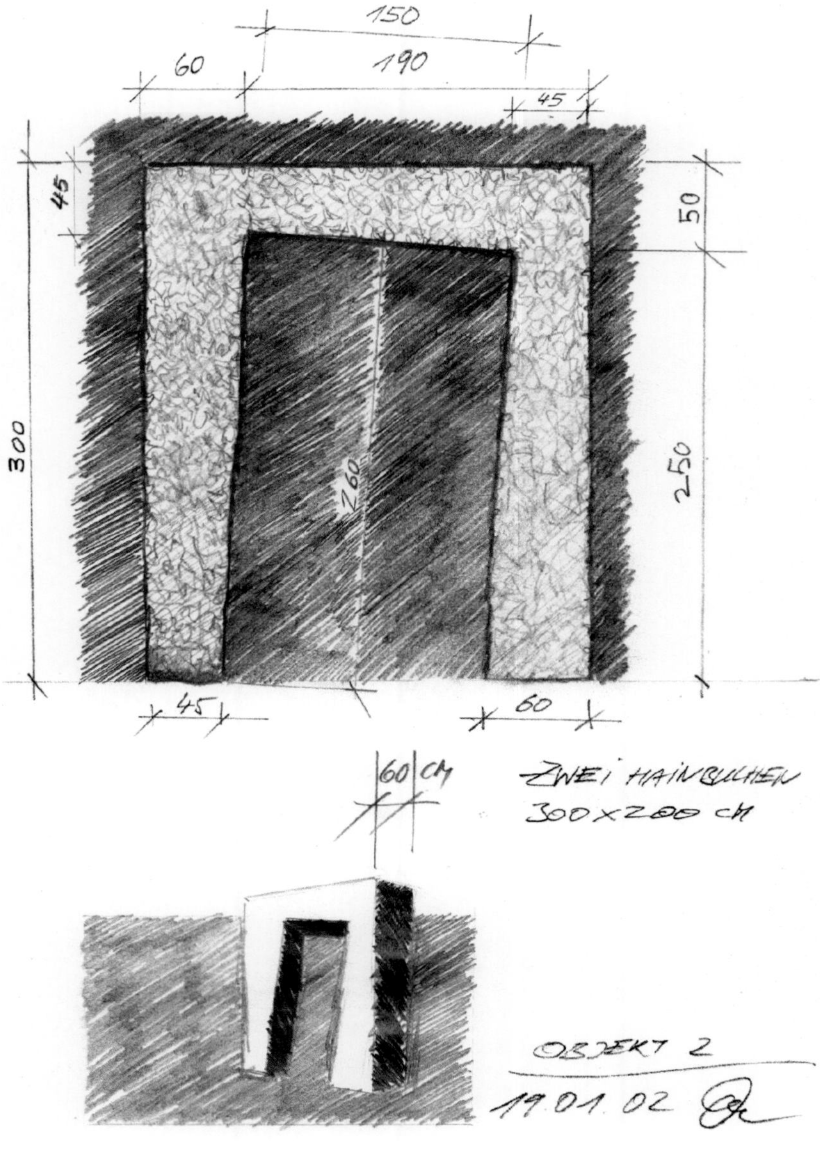

15. Var. 2
Plant Sculpture
2002

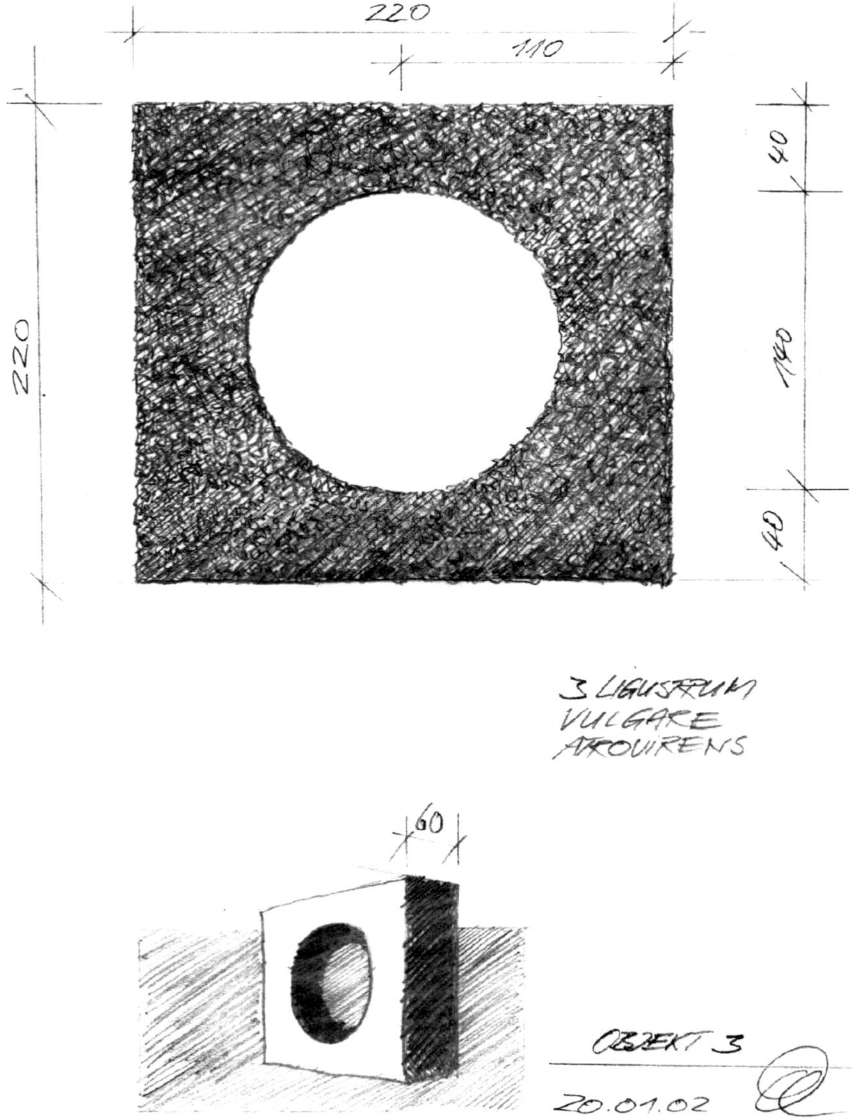

15. Var. 3
Plant Sculpture
2002

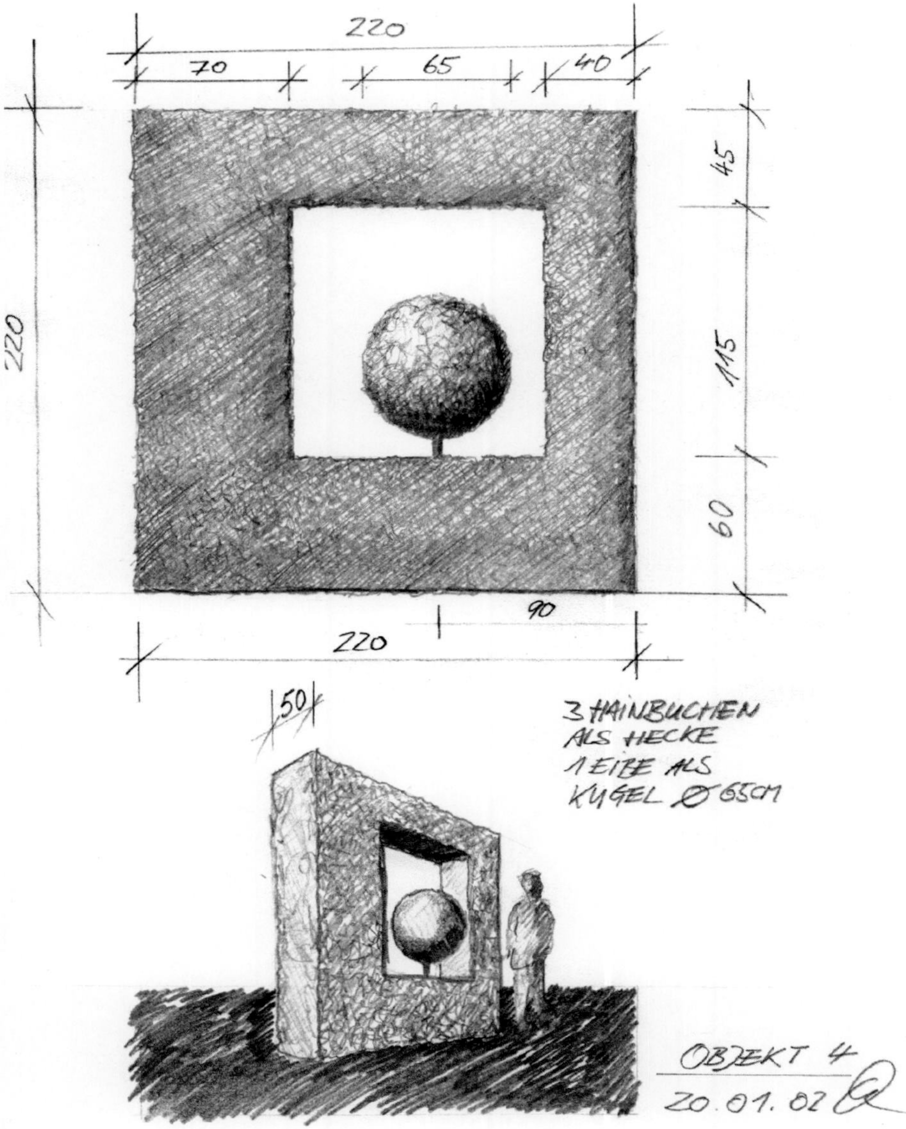

15. Var. 4
Plant Sculpture
2002

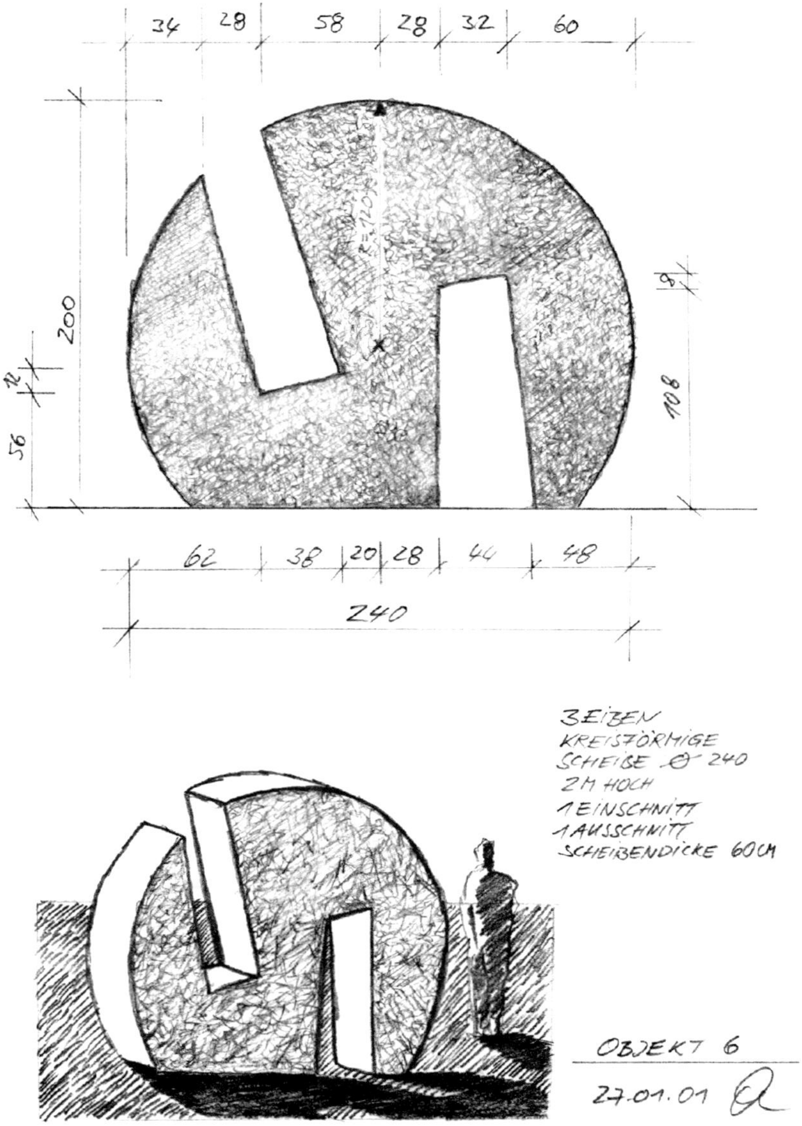

15. Var. 6
Plant Sculpture
2001

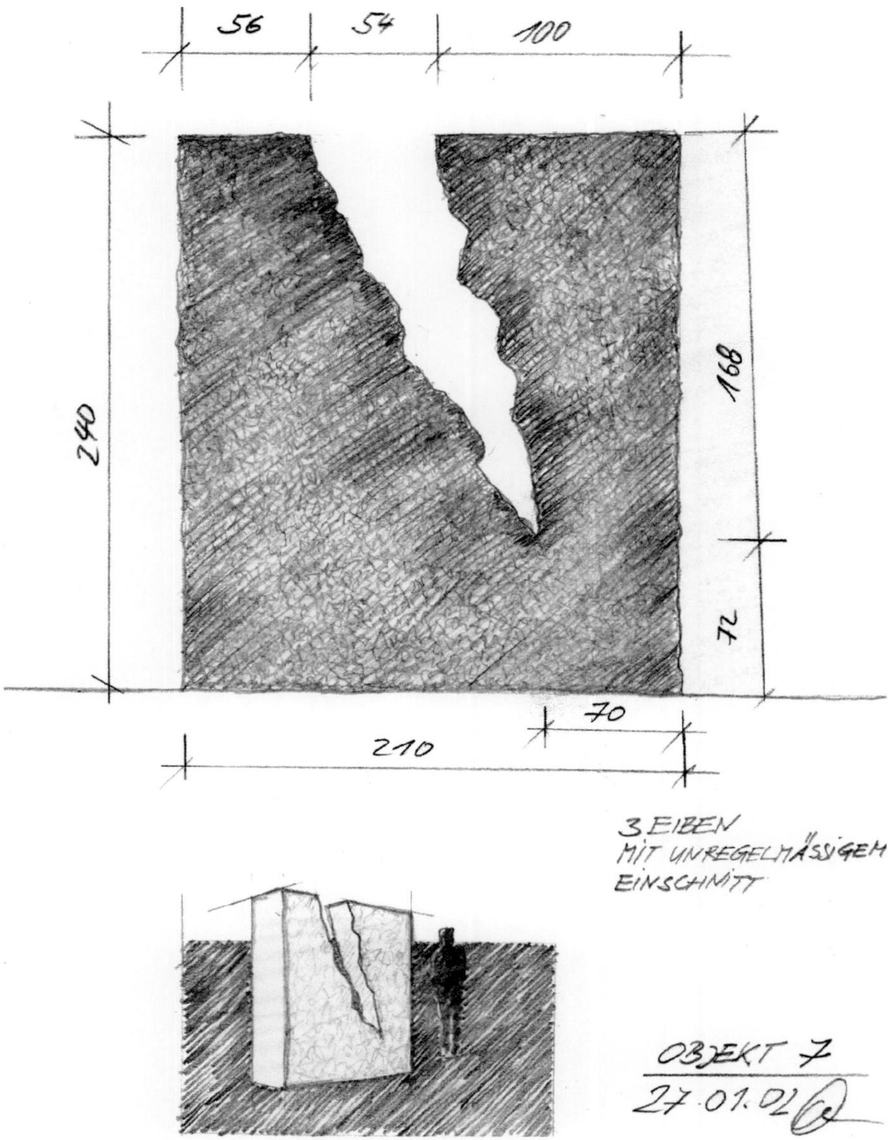

15. Var. 7
Plant Sculpture
2002

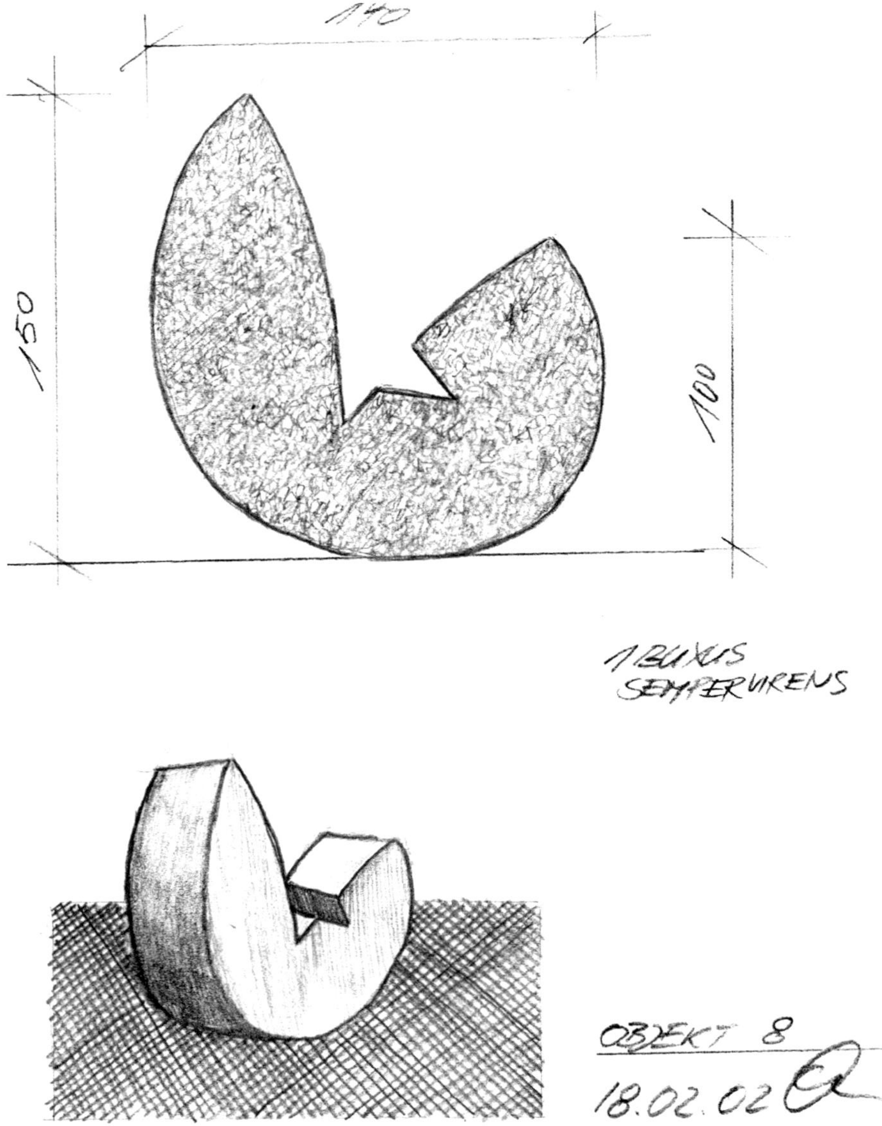

15. Var. 8
Plant Sculpture
2002

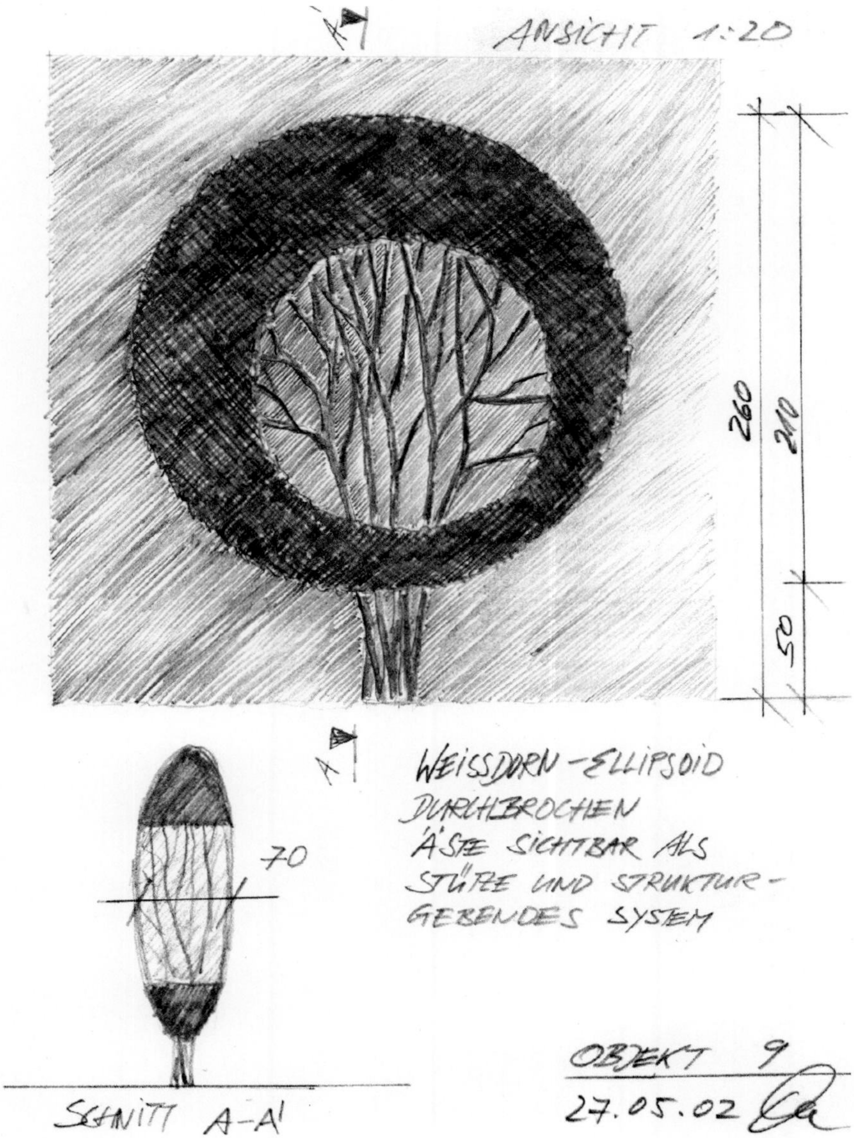

15. Var. 9
Plant Sculpture
2002

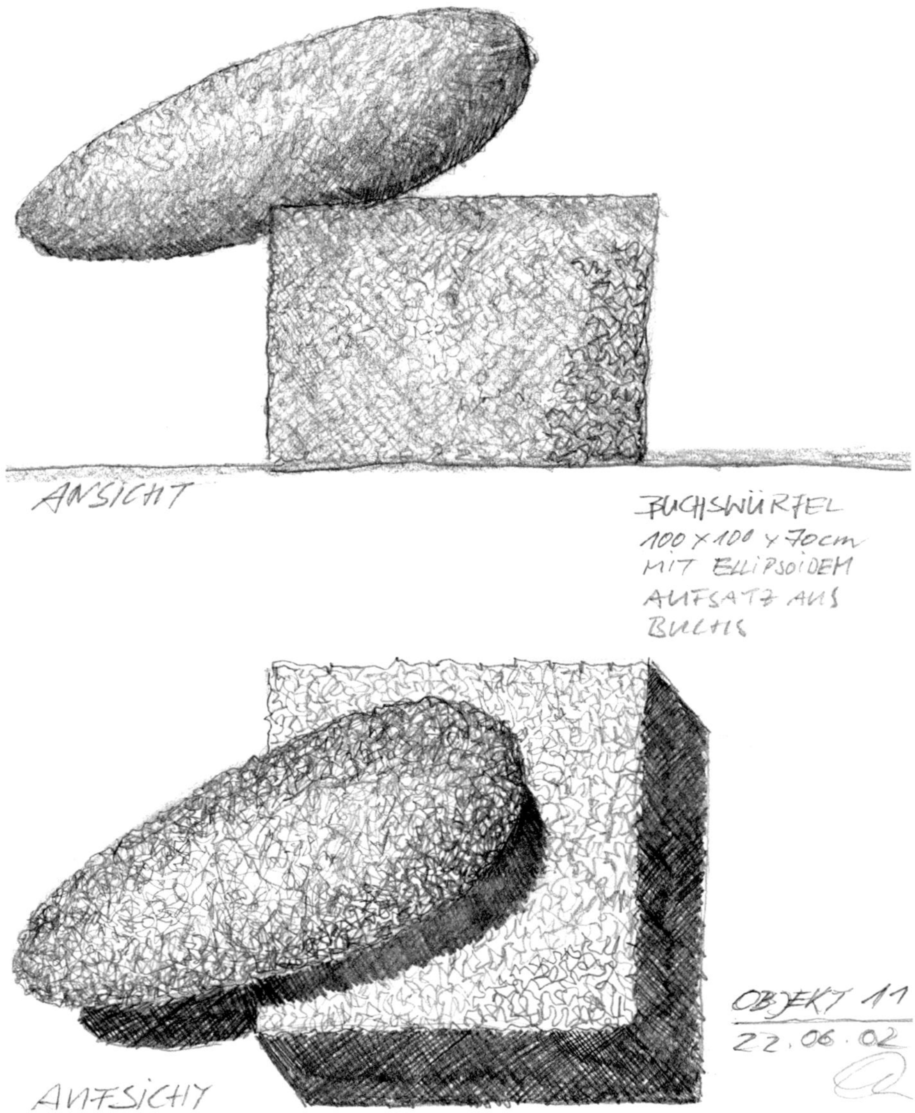

15. Var. 11
Plant Sculpture
2002

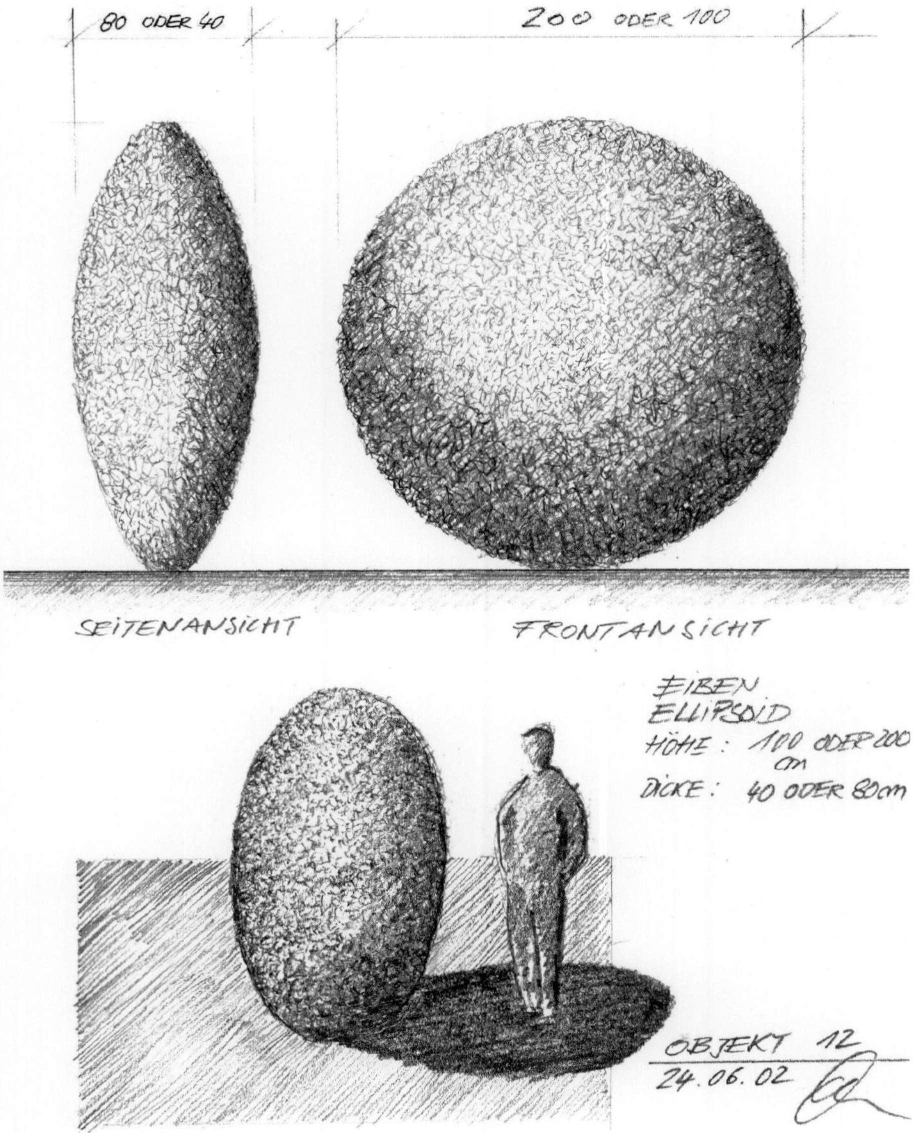

15. Var. 12
Plant Sculpture
2002

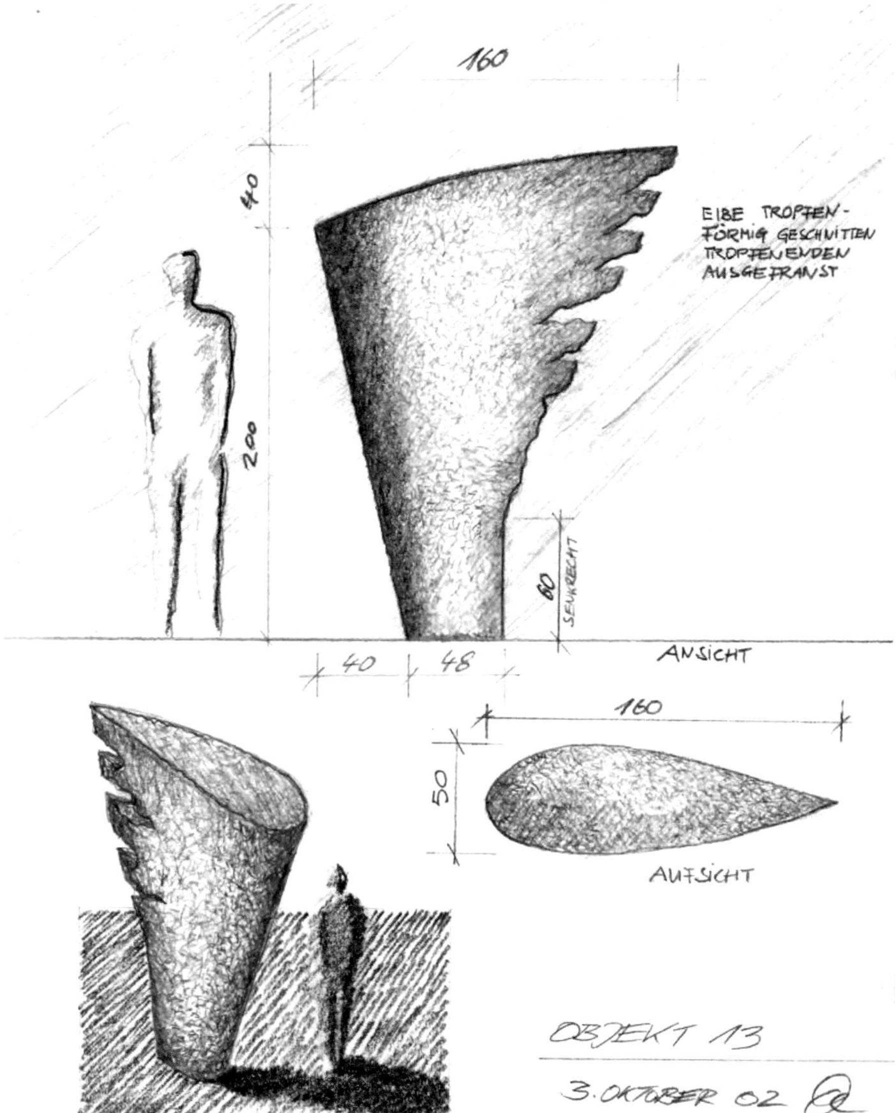

15. Var. 13
Plant Sculpture
2002

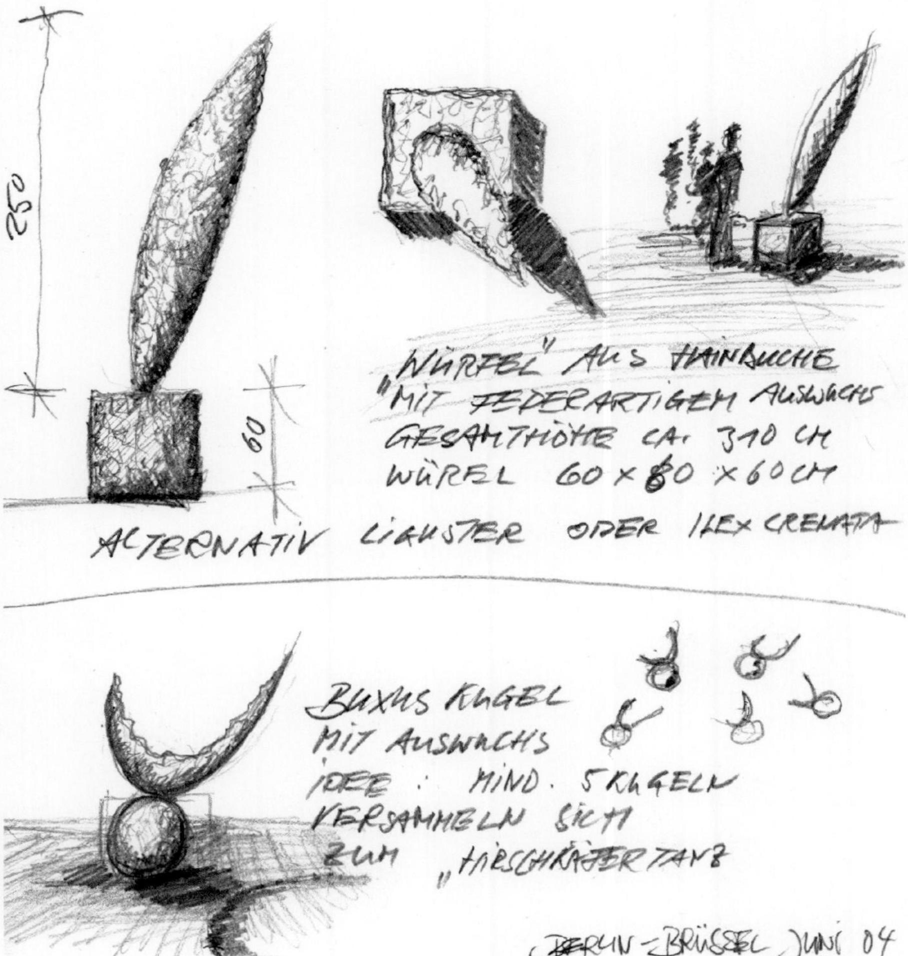

16
Plant Sculpture
Quill
2004

17
Plant Sculpture
Stag Beetle Ball
2004

Friedrich Küchelbecker: The Lime Tree in Donndorf near Bayreuth. Lithograph, around 1840. Gartenkunst-Museum Schloss Fantaisie, Eckersdorf near Bayreuth

18. Var. 1
Eurobonsai
2005

18. Var. 2–5
Eurobonsai
2005

18. Var. 6
Eurobonsai
2005

19
Surrealistic
Stone-Plant Sculpture
2001–2002

19.A and B
Photographs of the realized
Stone-Plant Sculpture
diagonal view and detail
2002

Stone-Plant Sculptures

20.A
Photograph of the realized
Cone-shaped
Stone-Plant Sculpture
2002

20
Cone-shaped
Stone-Plant Sculpture
2002

21
Vertical Ellipsoid
2002

Stone-Plant Sculptures

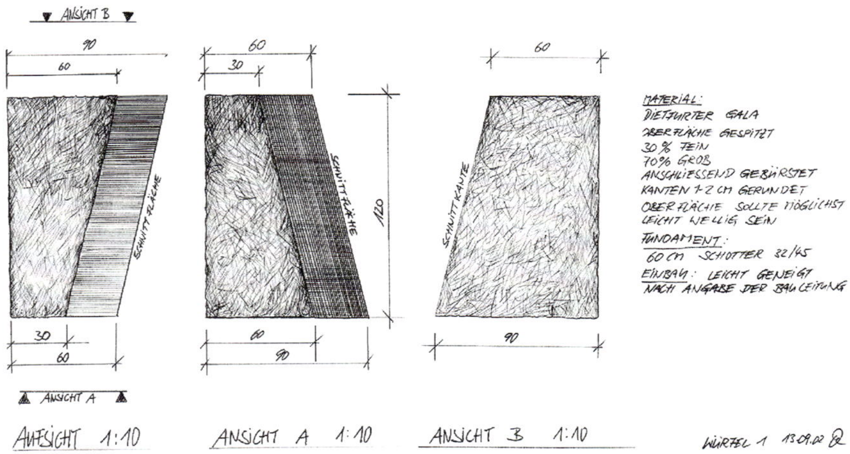

22
Cubic Stone-Plant
Sculpture
2002

22.A–D
Photographs of the realized
Stone-Plant Sculpture
2002

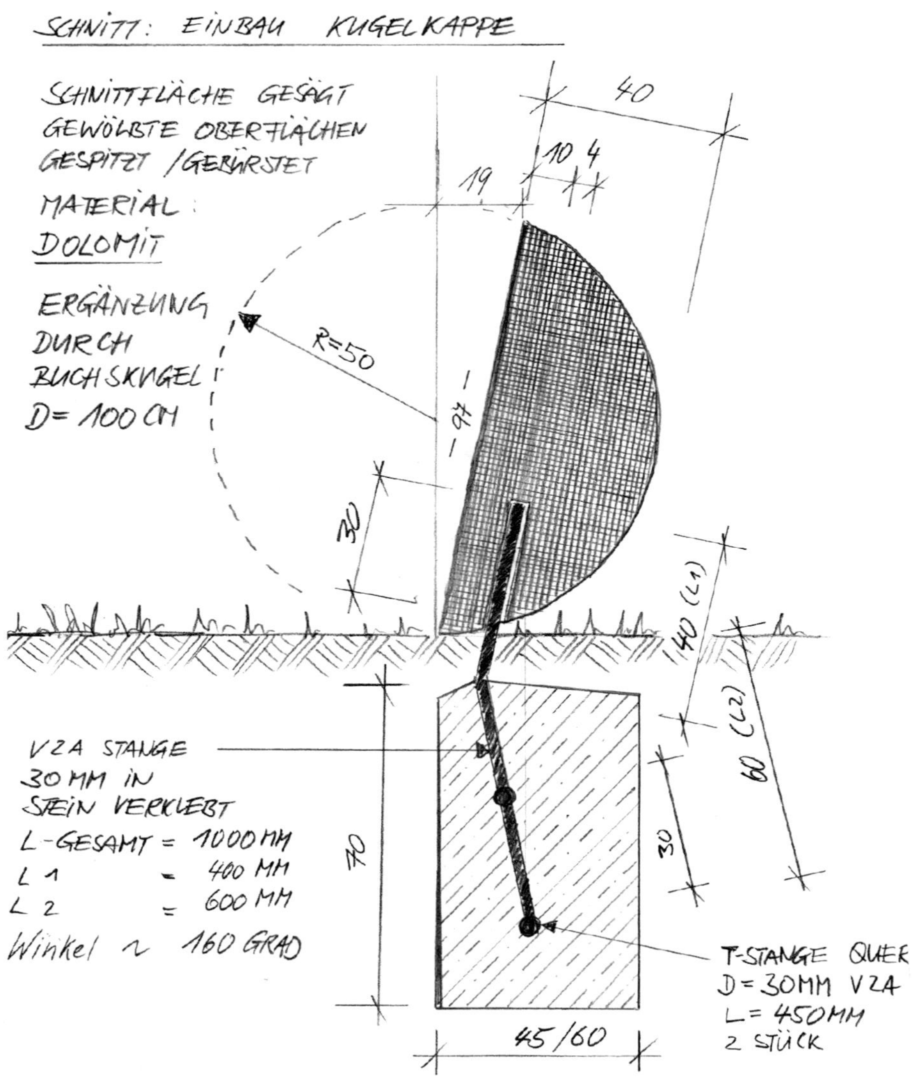
SCHNITT: EINBAU KUGELKAPPE
SCHNITTFLÄCHE GESÄGT
GEWÖLBTE OBERFLÄCHEN
GESPITZT /GEBÜRSTET
MATERIAL:
DOLOMIT
ERGÄNZUNG
DURCH
BUCHSKUGEL
D= 100 CM
R=50
40
10 4
19
94
30
40 (L1)
60 (L2)
70
30
45/60
V2A STANGE
30 MM IN
STEIN VERKLEBT
L-GESAMT = 1000 MM
L 1 = 400 MM
L 2 = 600 MM
Winkel ~ 160 GRAD
T-STANGE QUER
D= 30 MM V2A
L= 450 MM
2 STÜCK

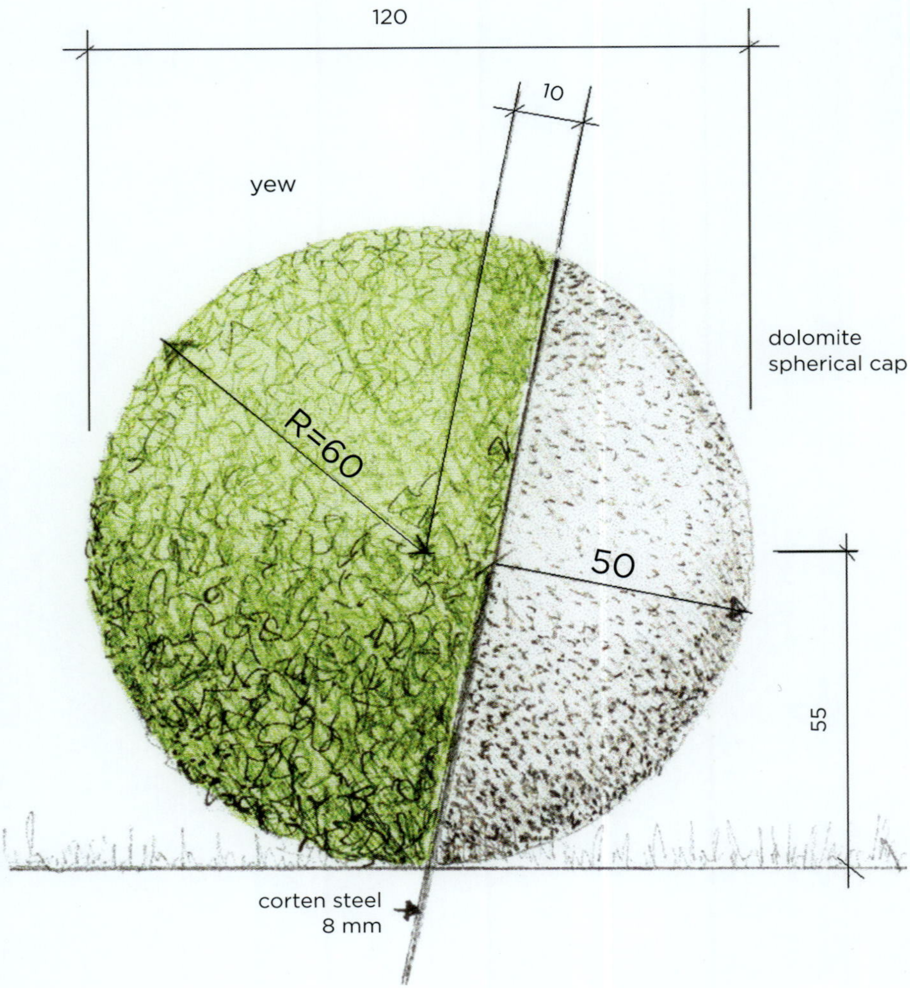

23.A
View of the realized
Stone-Plant Sculpture
2002

23
Ball-shaped
Stone-Plant Sculpture
2002

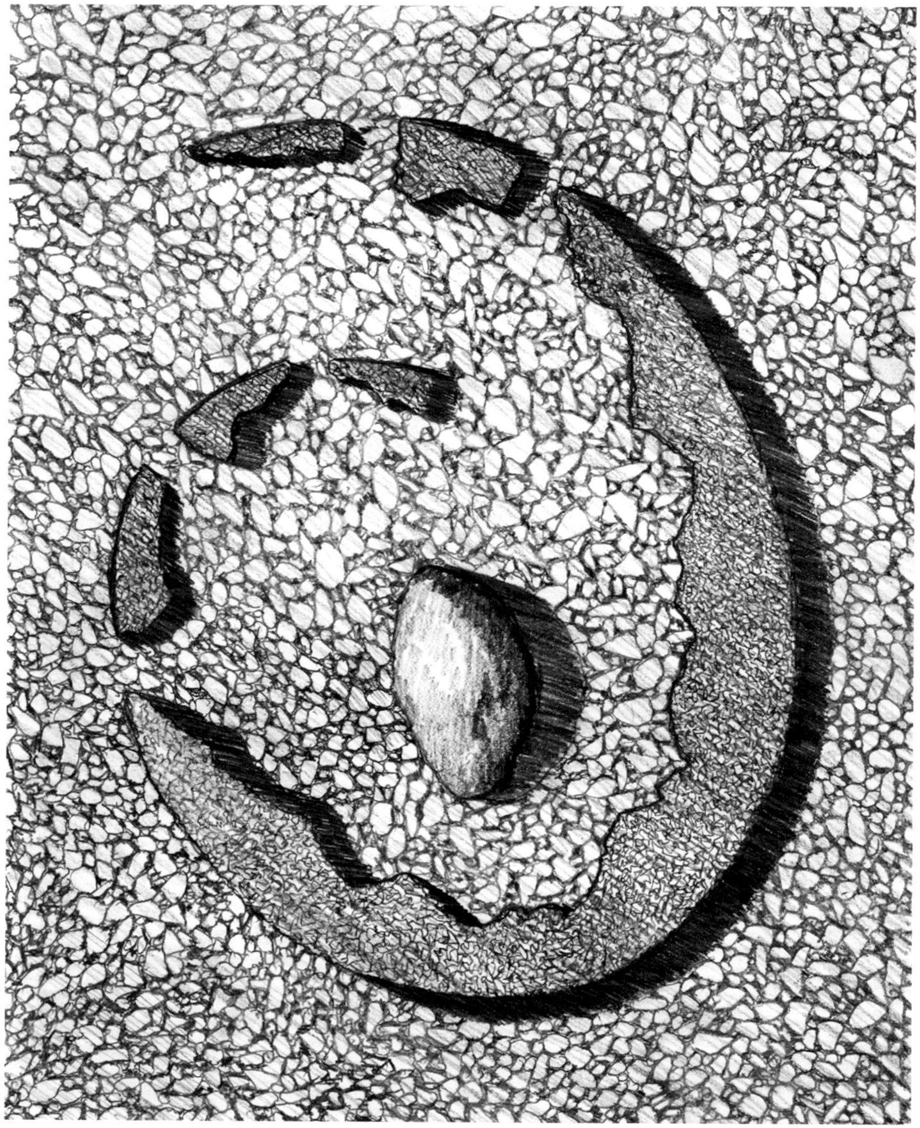

24
Ariadne's Thread
2003

24.A–C
Photographs of
the realized labyrinth
2003

Stone-Plant Sculptures

25
Halved Erratic Blocks
Interwoven with Willows
2005–2006

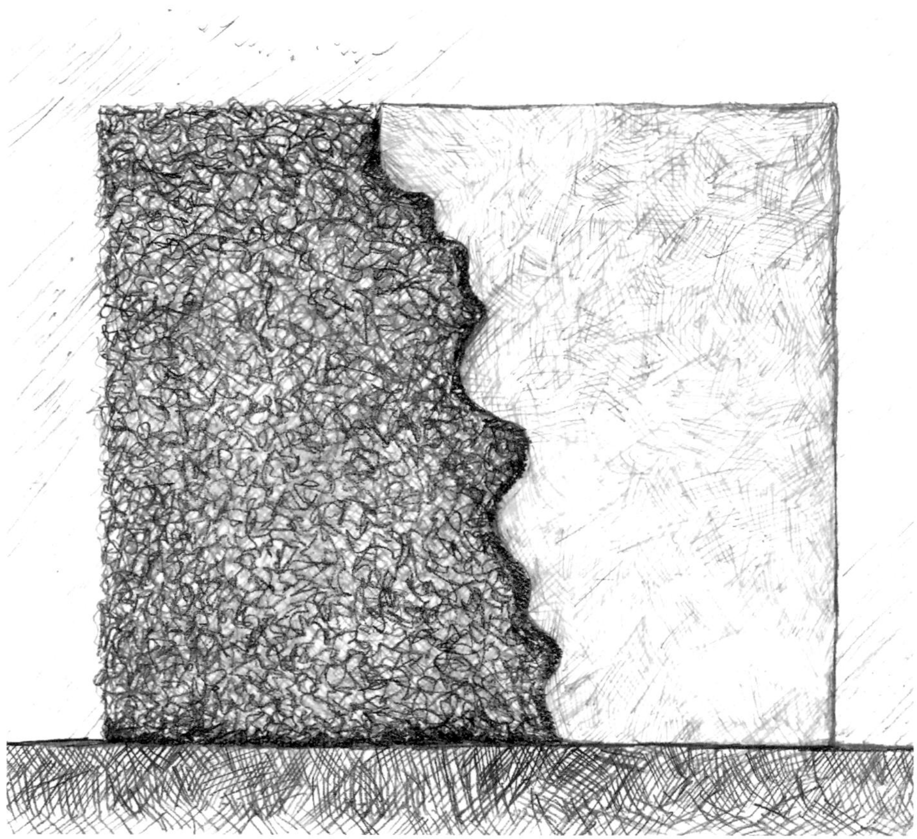

26
Rectangular Cube
2006

26.A and B
Photographs of the realized
Rectangular Cube
2006

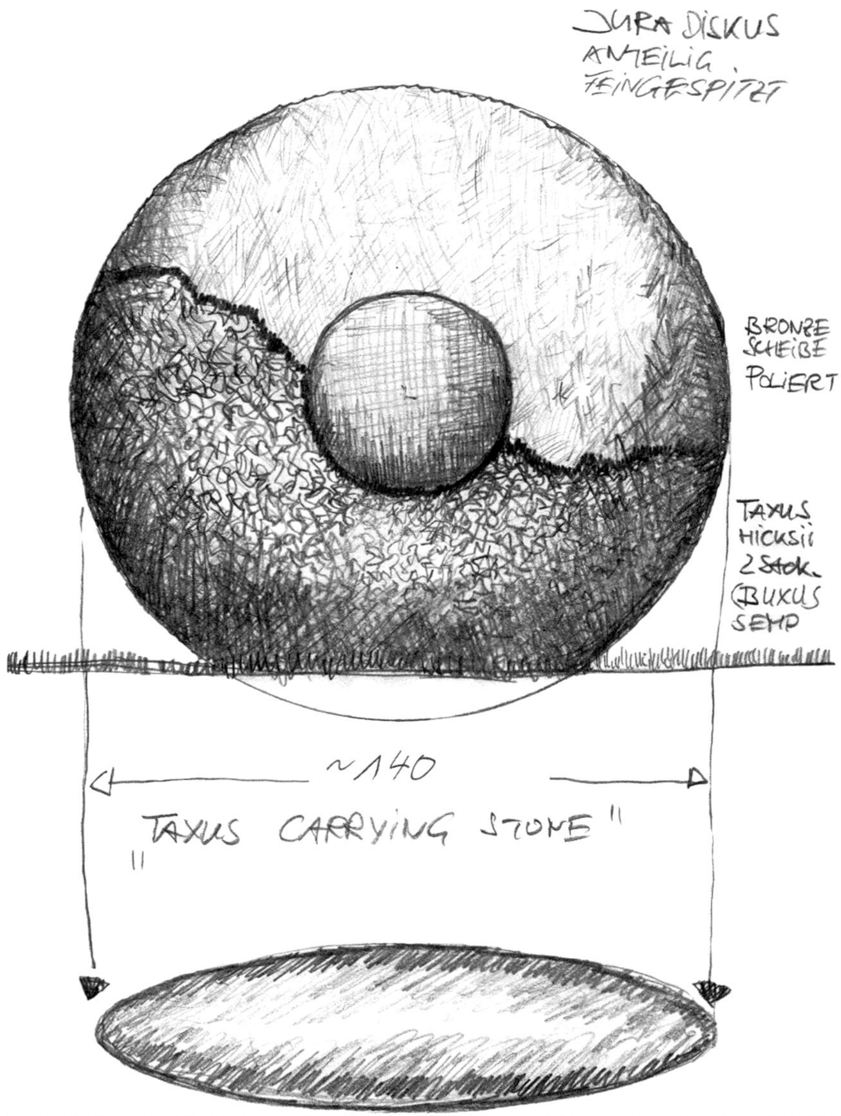
JURA DISKUS
ANTEILIG
FEINGESPITZT
BRONZE
SCHEIBE
POLIERT
TAXUS
HICKSII
2 STCK.
BUXUS
SEMP
~140
"TAXUS CARRYING STONE"

Stone-Plant Sculptures

27.A
Photograph of the realized
Flying Stone Discus
2008

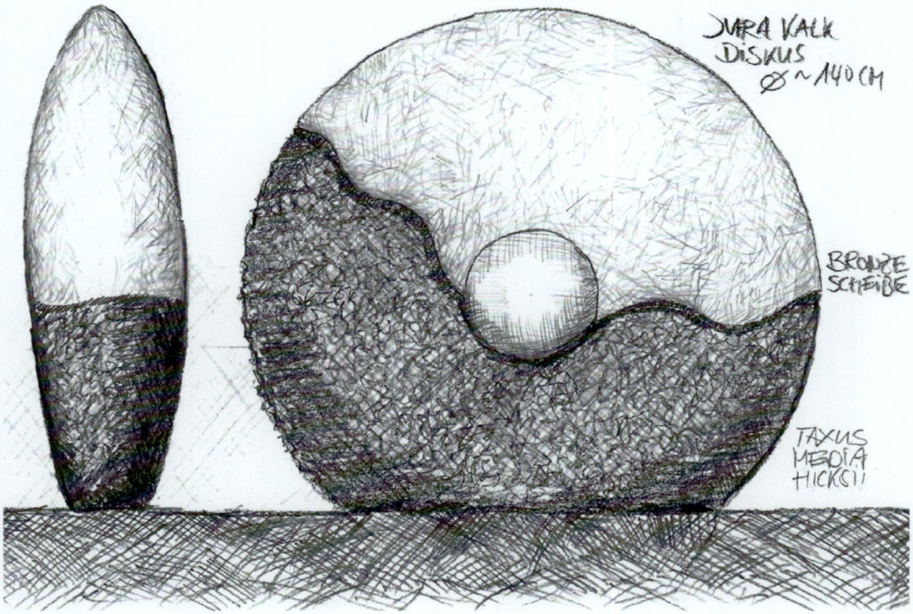

27
Flying Stone Discus
2008

Other Sculptures

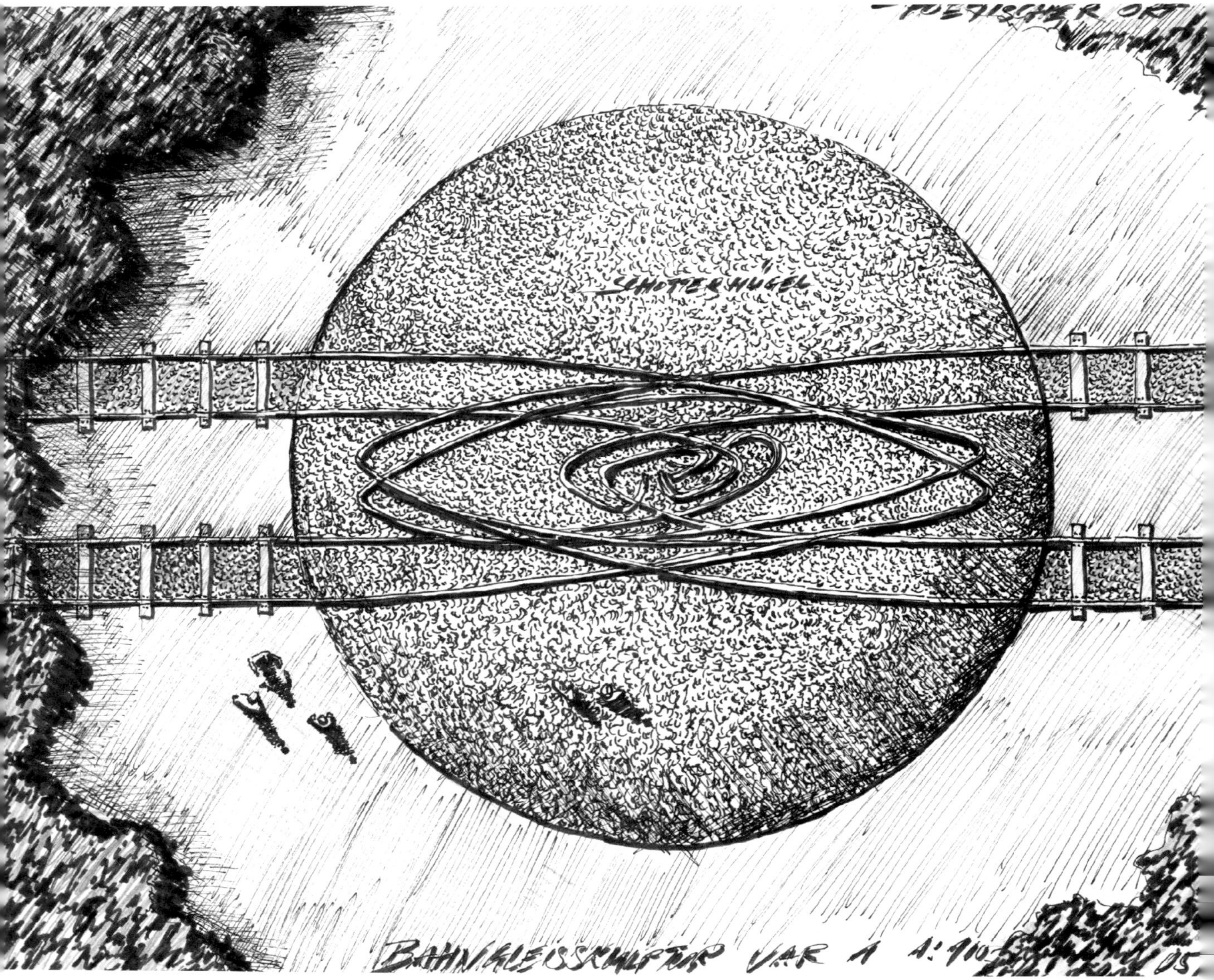

28
Railway Track Sculpture
2006/2008

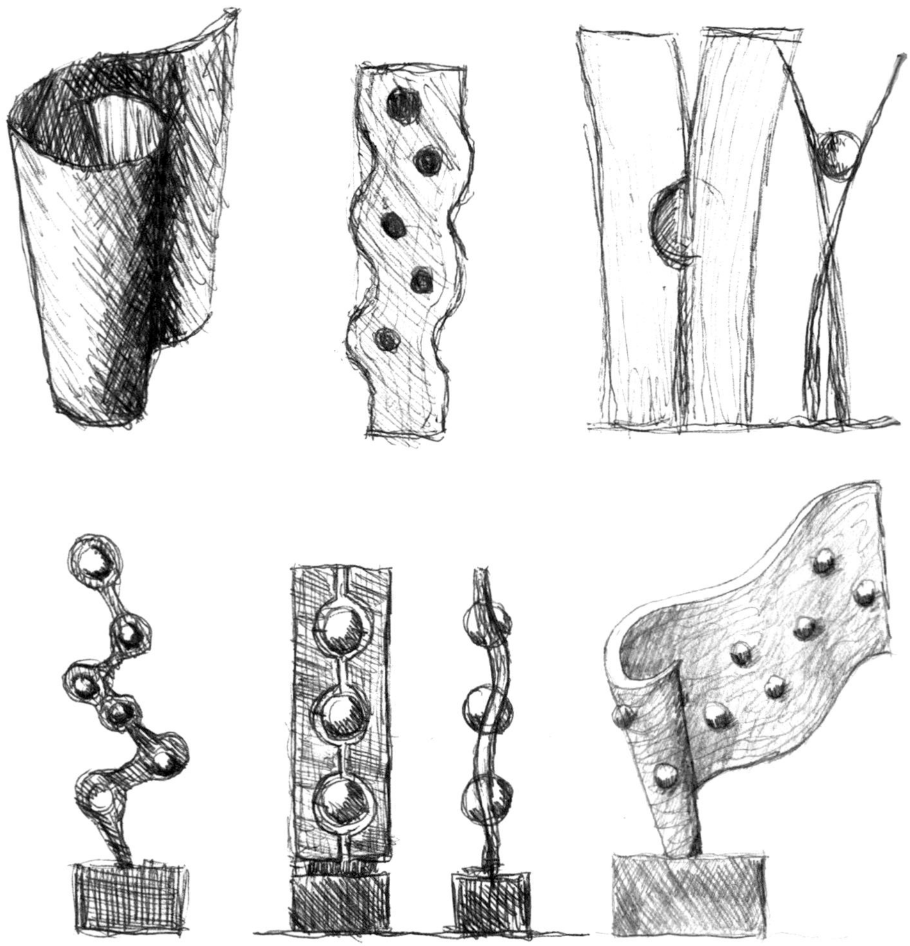

29. Var. 1–6
Ideas for
an Award Trophy
Green Music Award
2007

30
Steel Nest
for Pine Trunks
2009

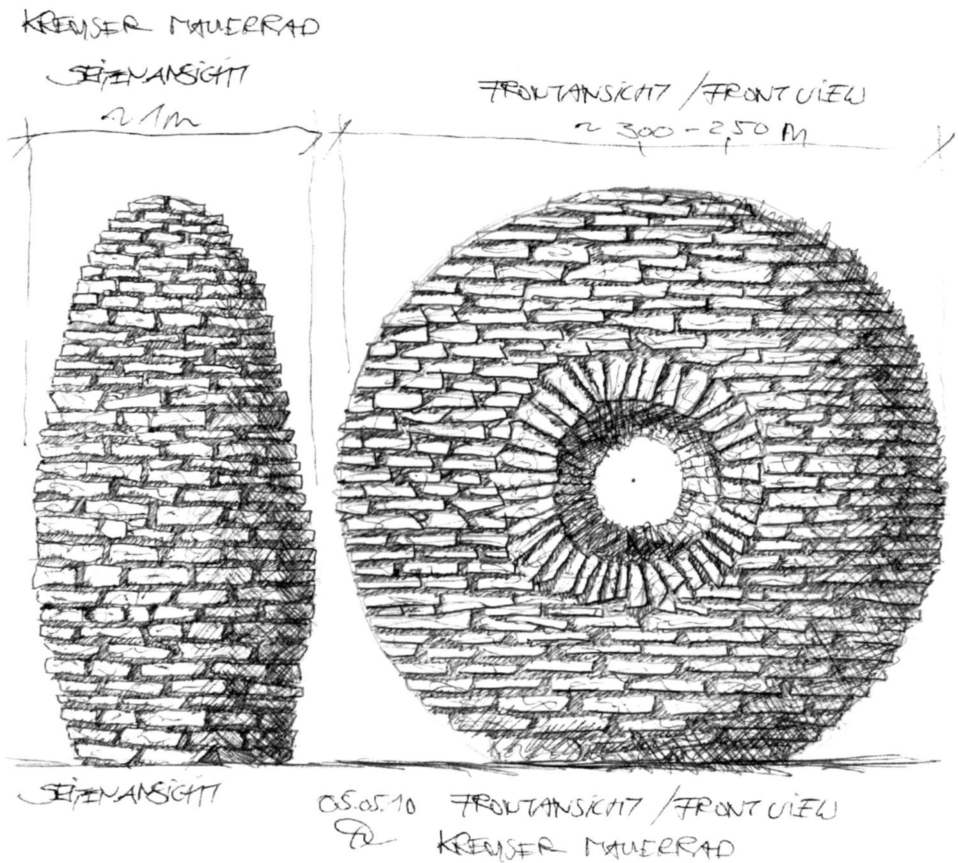

31.1
Stone Object
Krems Wall Wheel
2010

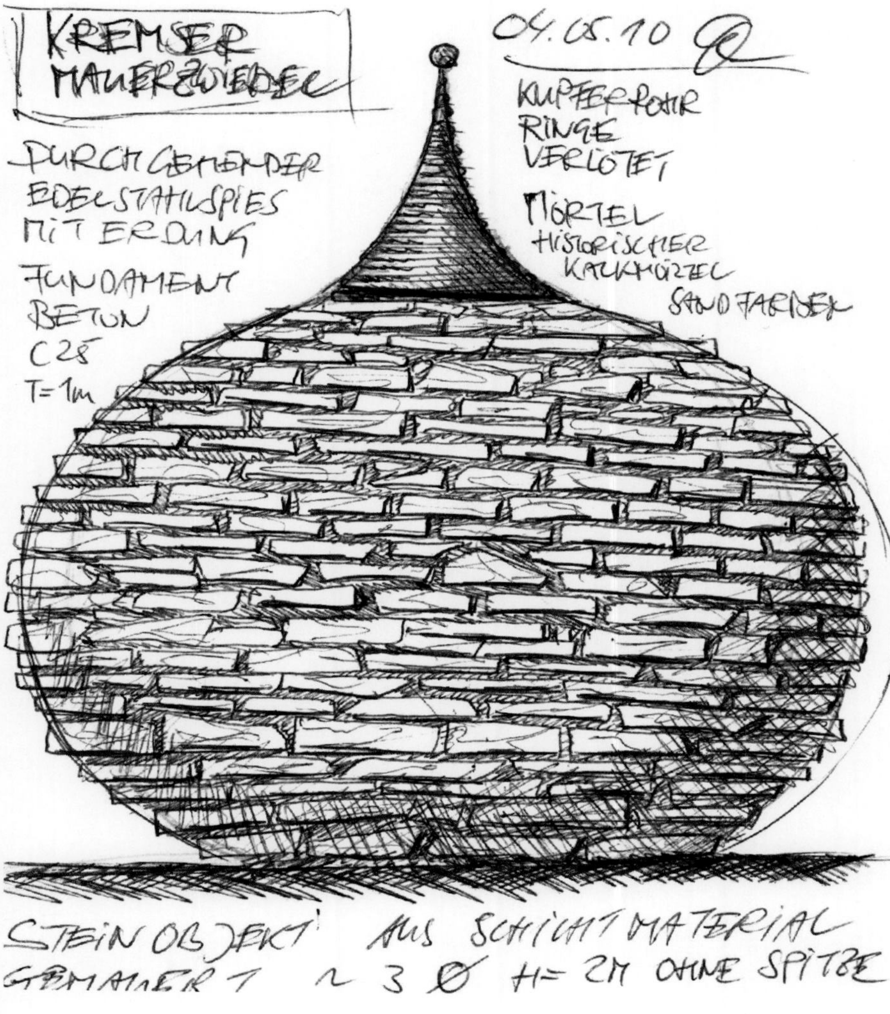

31.2
Stone Object
Krems Wall Onion
2010

32
Stage Design for a Sculpture of the Commendatore (Don Giovanni)
2010

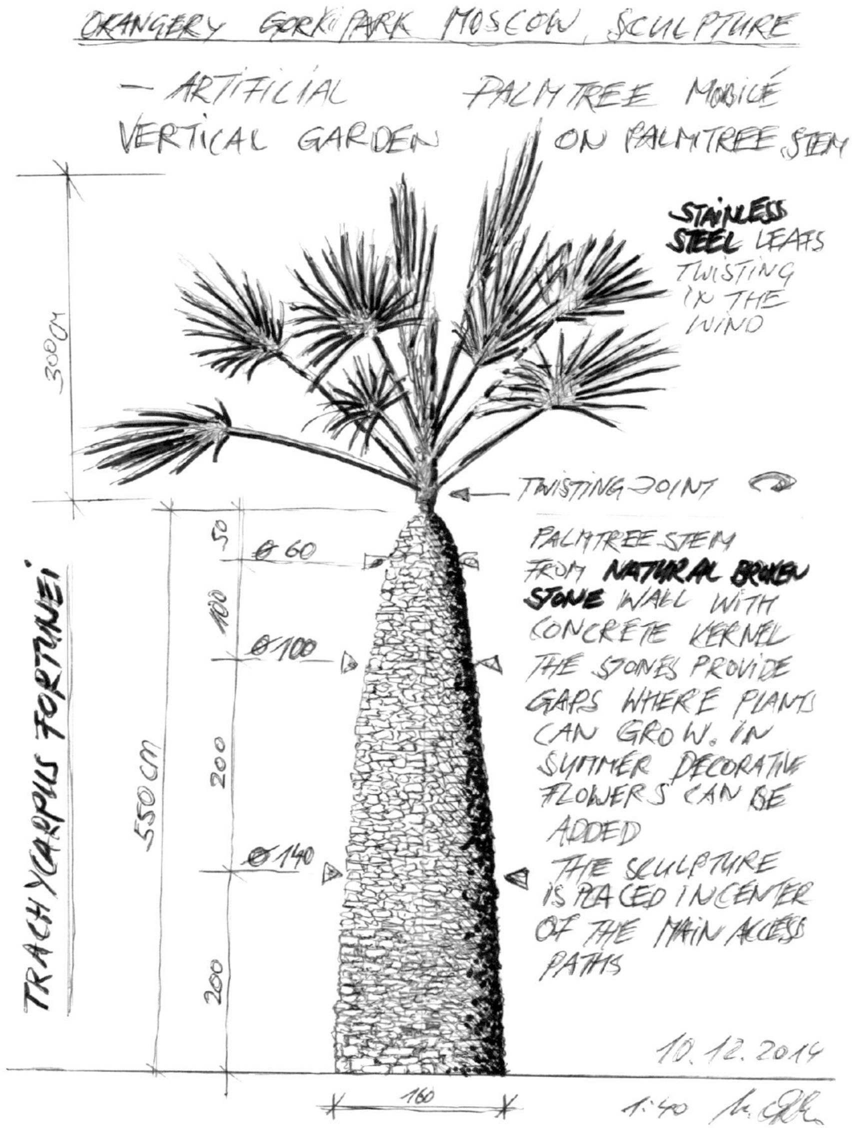

33.1
Palm Tree
Mobile Sculpture
2014

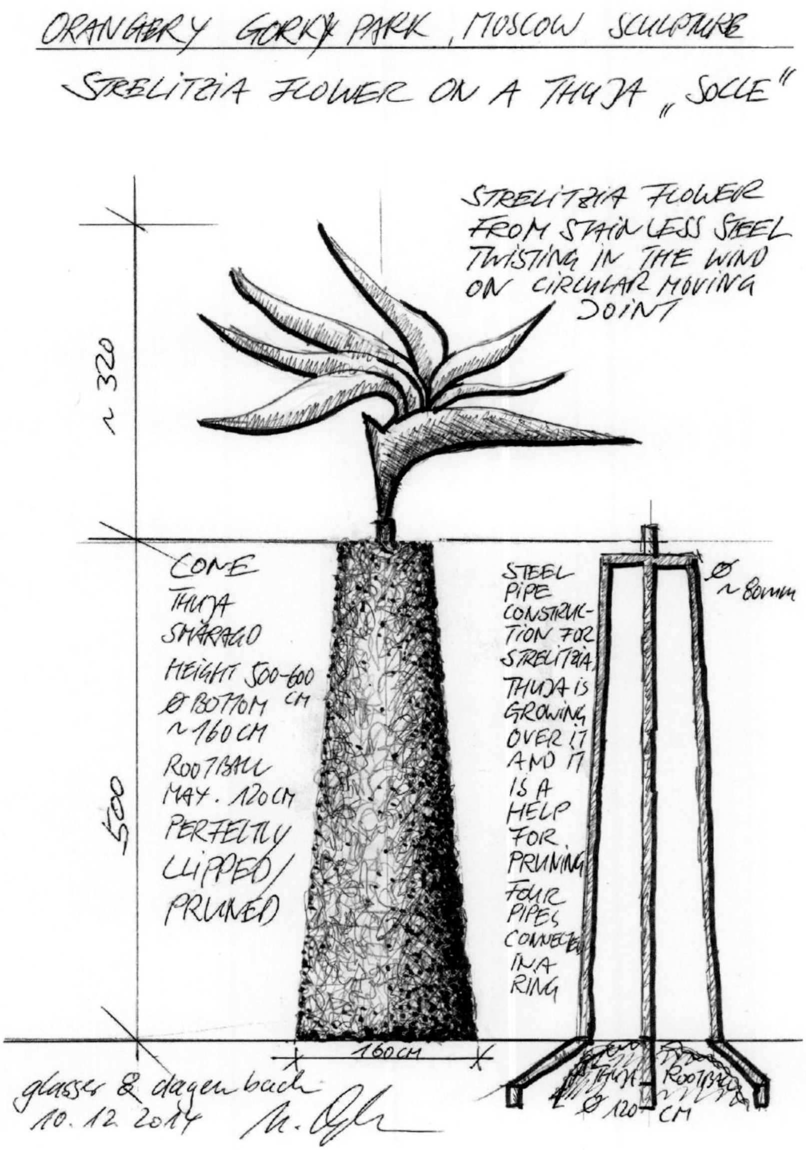

33.2
Strelitzia
Mobile Sculpture
2014

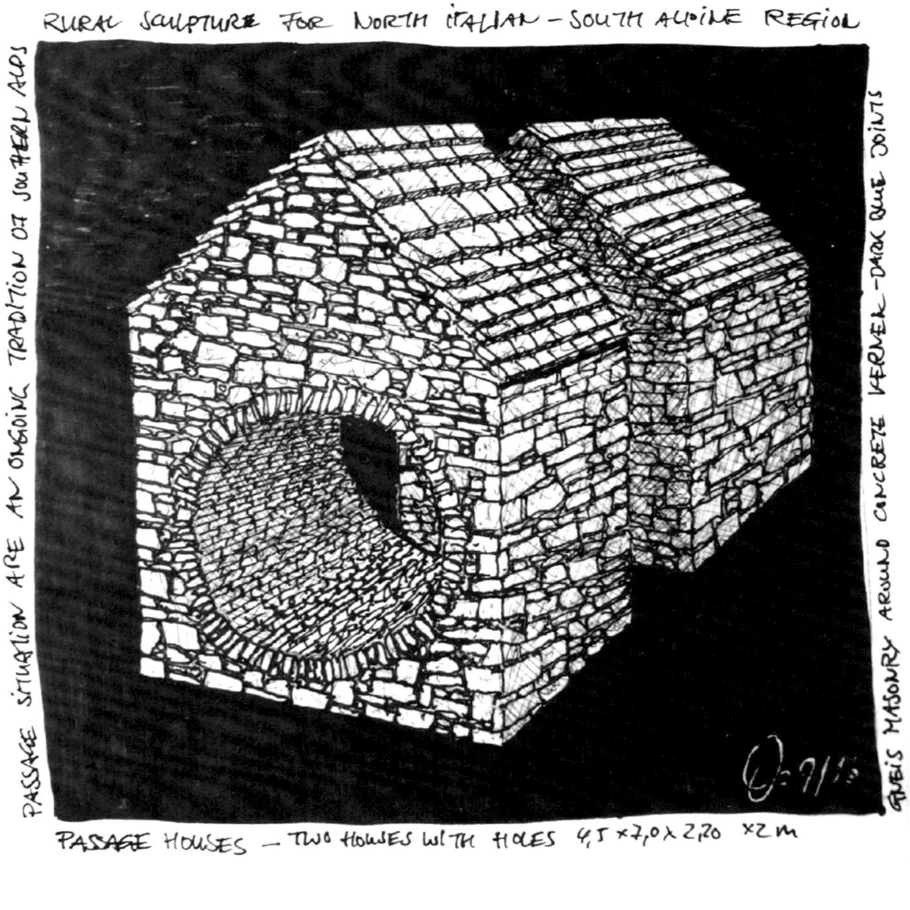
RURAL SCULPTURE FOR NORTH ITALIAN – SOUTH ALPINE REGION
PASSAGE SITUATION ARE AN ONGOING TRADITION OF SOUTHERN ALPS
GNEIS MASONRY AROUND CONCRETE KERNEL – DARK BLUE JOINTS
PASSAGE HOUSES – TWO HOUSES WITH HOLES 4,5 x 7,0 x 2,20 x 2 m

34. Var. 1 and 2
Gneissic Rock Houses
2016

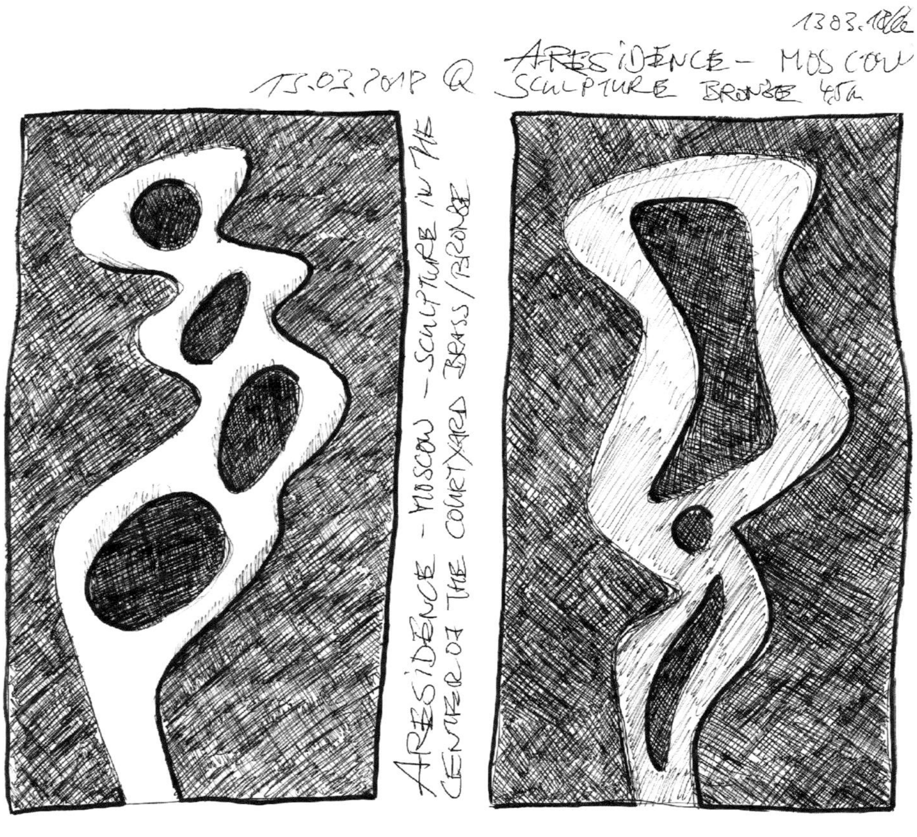

35. Var. 1–3
Amorphous Aluminium
Sculptures
2018

Other Sculptures

35.A
3D print model
of the sculpture
2019

LANDSCAPE ACHITECTURE +COMPETITIONS

Competitions

Show Gardens + Exhibitions

Landscape Architecture

AUSSICHTSTURM AN DER SCHWIERSBERGALM 06.02.2010

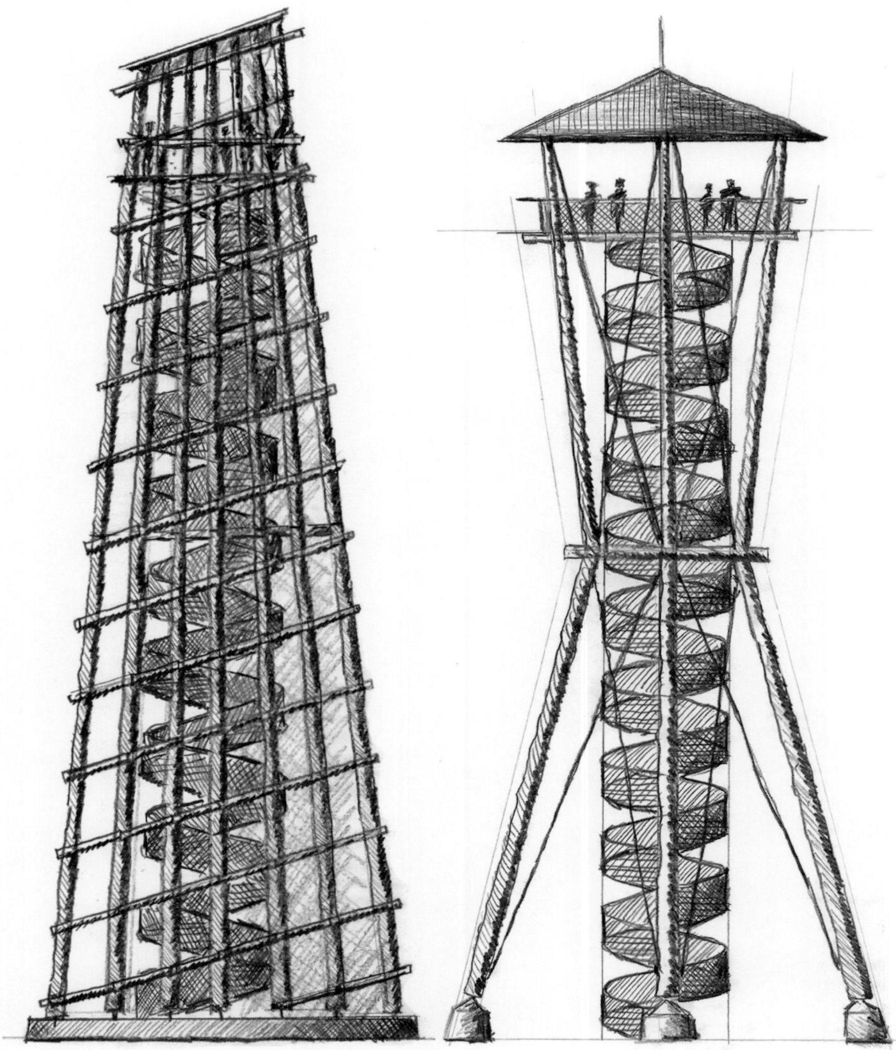

36. Var. 1–3
Three Proposals for
an Observation Tower
2010

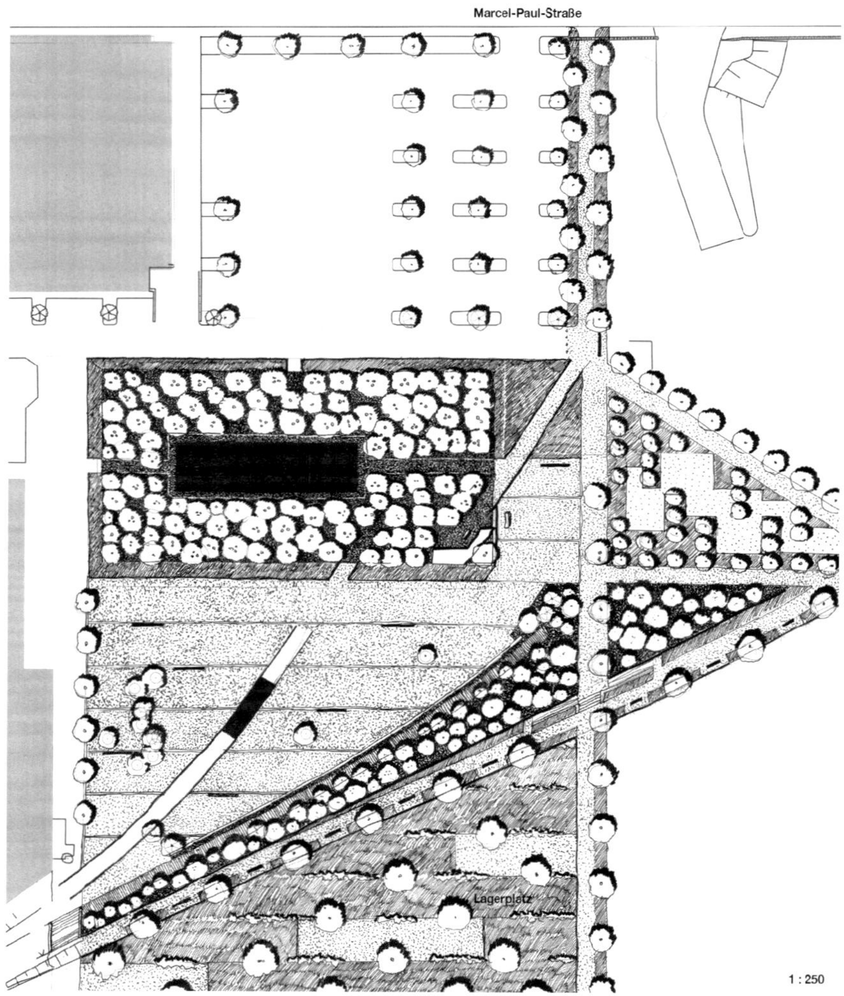

37
Former Cattle Auction Hall
Memorial for deported and murdered Thuringian Jews
2018

37.1
site plan

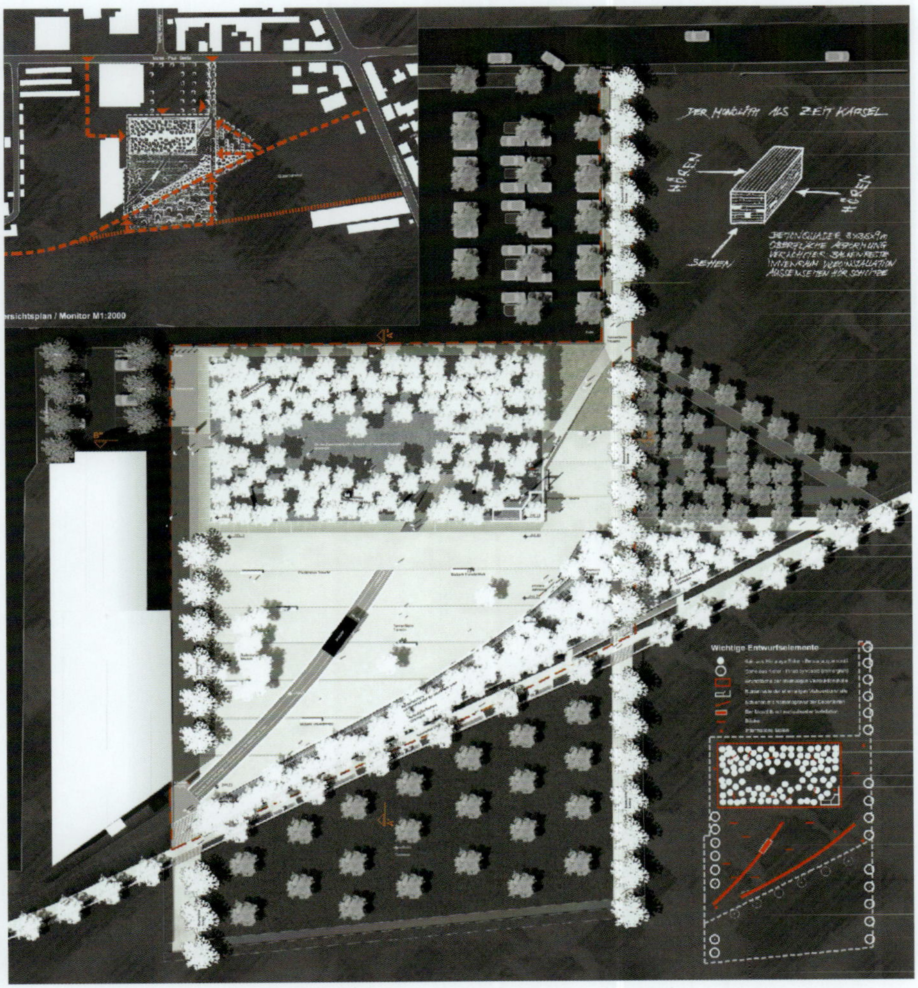

37.A
Site plan, mixed media

Section A'A"

Section B'B"

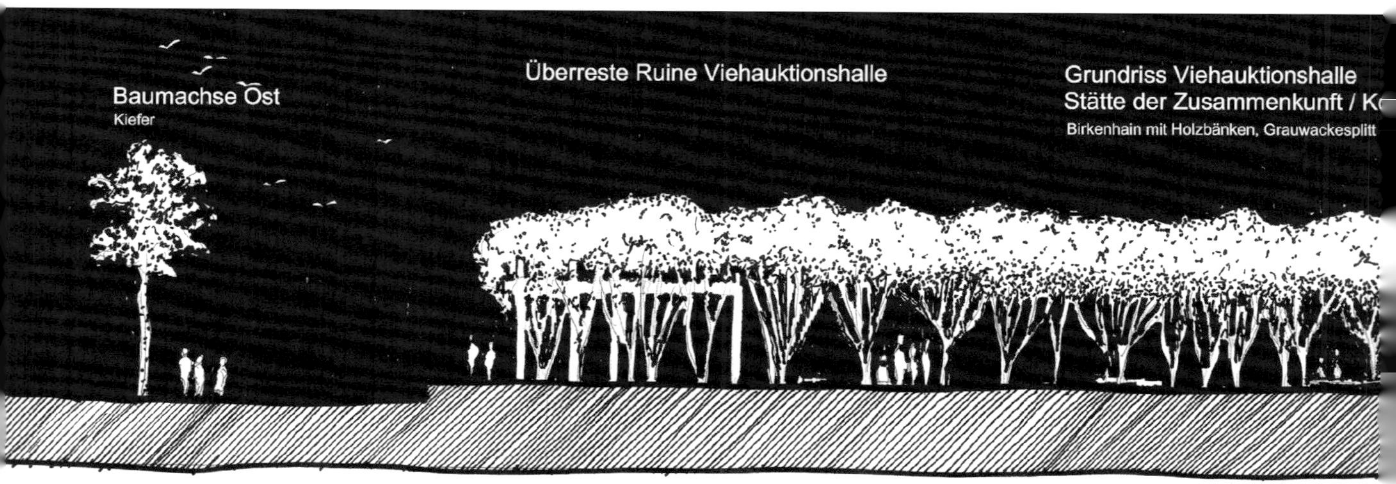

37.2 and 3
Sectional illustrations

EHEMALIGE
VIEH
AUKTIONS
HALLE
DIE ÜBERRESTE
GEDENKORT
ZUR
DEPORTATION
DER
THÜRINGER
JUDEN

37.4
Illustration
with information board

— DER MONOLITH — WEIMAR WETTBEWERB 2018 GEDENKORT ZUR DEPORTATION DER WEIMARER JUDEN 15.01.18 M.Q

37.5–6
Sectional illustrations showing the monolith

38.A
Inside view of the
realized garden
2013

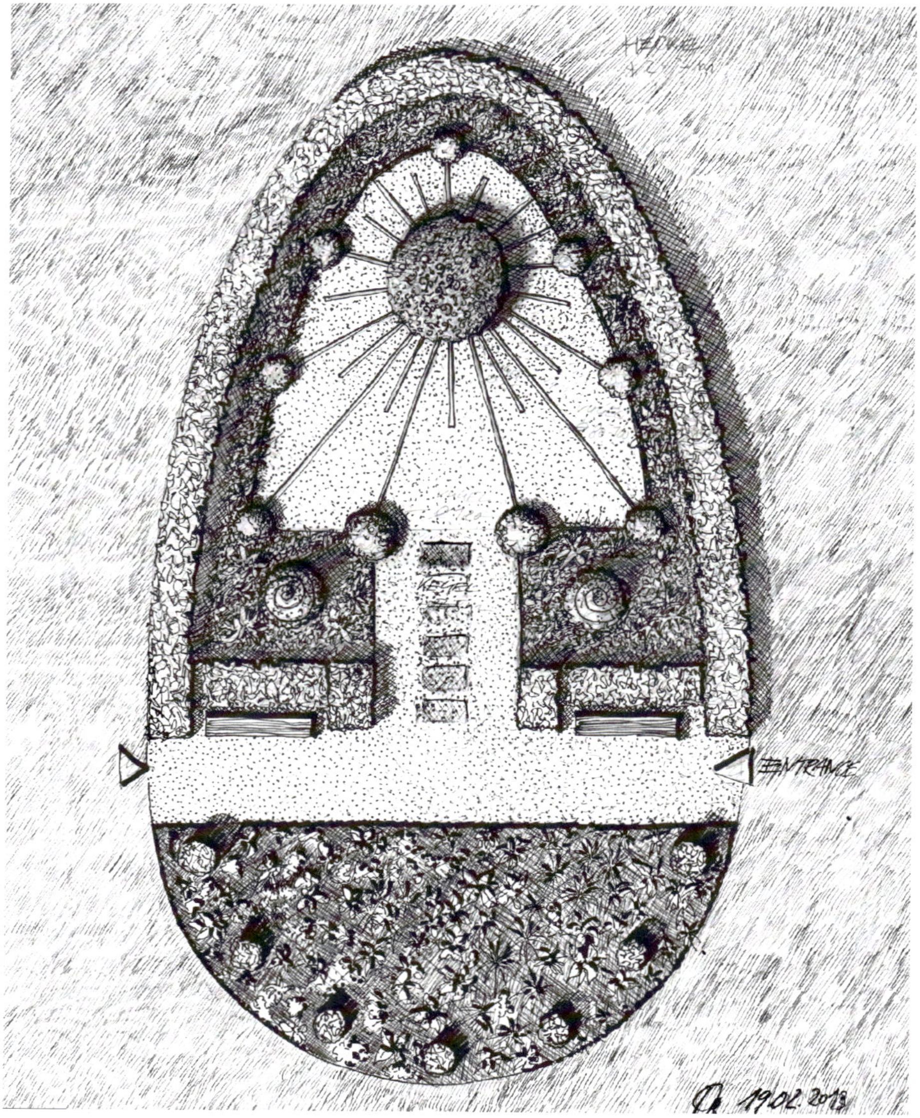

38
Fabergé Egg Garden
2013

38.B and C
Rendering: top view
and detail

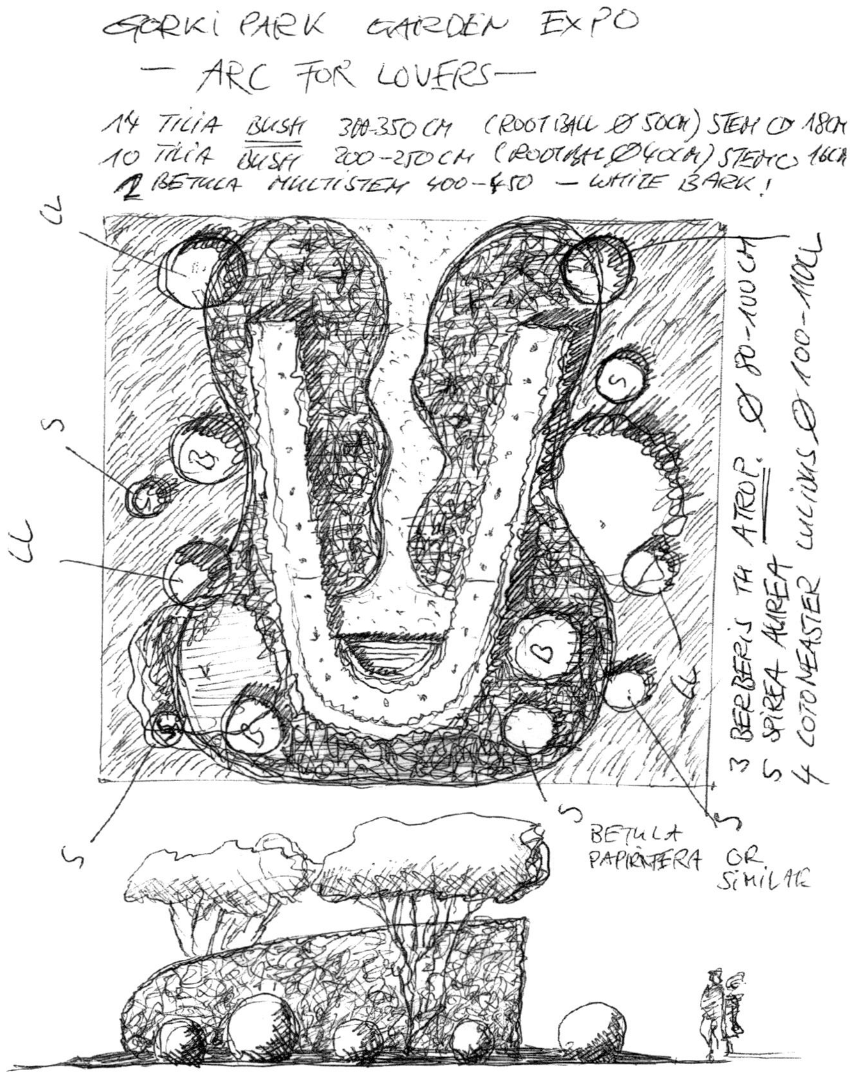
GORKI PARK GARDEN EXPO
— ARC FOR LOVERS —
14 TILIA BUSH 300-350 CM (ROOTBALL Ø 50CM) STEM Ø 18CM
10 TILIA BUSH 200-250 CM (ROOTBALL Ø 40CM) STEM Ø 16CM
2 BETULA MULTISTEM 400-450 — WHITE BARK!
3 BERBERIS TH ATROP. Ø 80-100 CM
5 SPIREA AUREA
4 COTONEASTER LUCIDUS Ø 100-110CM
BETULA PAPIRIFERA OR SIMILAR

39.A
Inside view
of the realized arc
2014

39.1–2
Arc for Lovers
2014

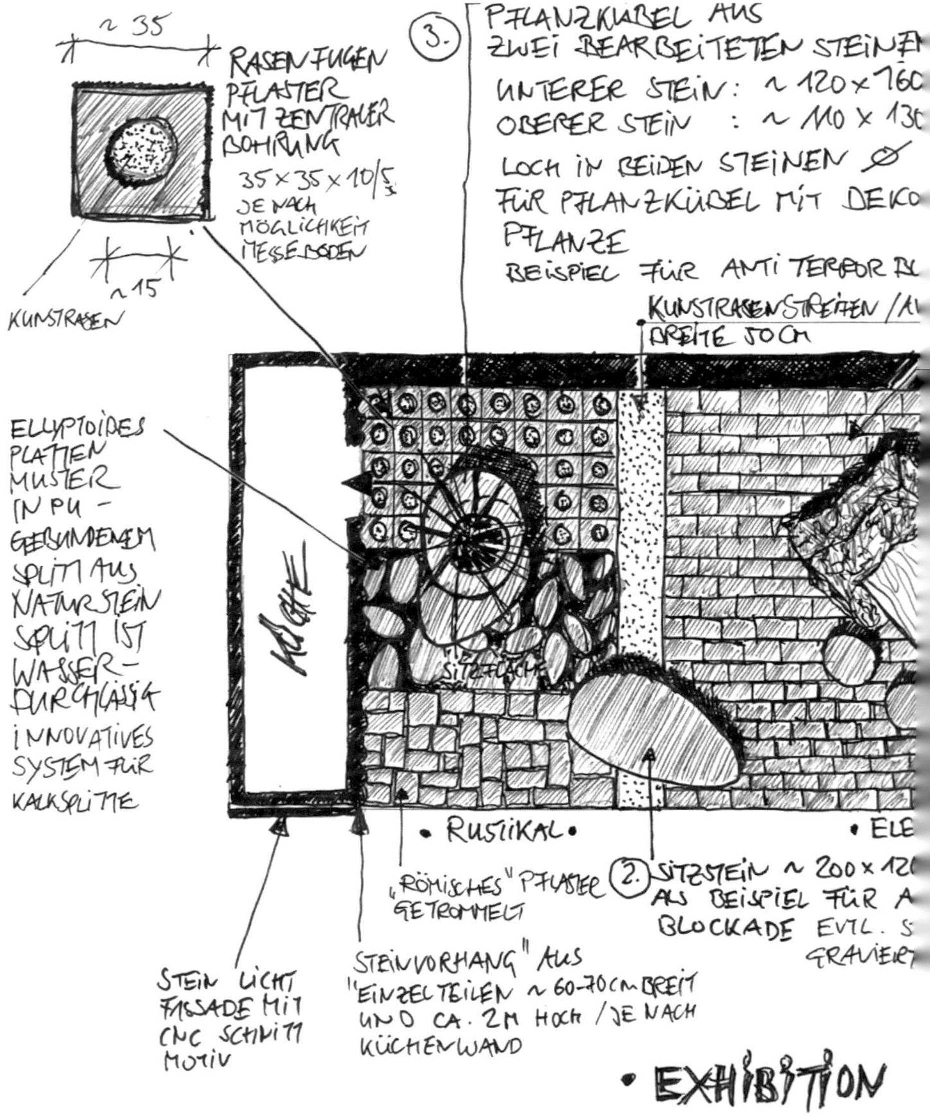
~ 35
RASENFUGEN PFLASTER MIT ZENTRALER BOHRUNG
35 x 35 x 10/5
JE NACH MÖGLICHKEIT MESSEBODEN
~ 15
KUNSTRASEN
3.
PFLANZKÜBEL AUS
LOCH IN BEIDEN STEINEN Ø
PFLANZE
ELLYPTOIDES PLATTEN MUSTER IN PU-GEBUNDENEM SPLITT AUS NATURSTEIN SPLITT IST WASSERDURCHLÄSSIG
INNOVATIVES SYSTEM FÜR KALKSPLITTE
KÜCHE
SITZFLÄCHE
• RUSTIKAL •
„RÖMISCHES" PFLASTER GETROMMELT
2.
STEIN LICHT FASSADE MIT CNC SCHNITT MOTIV
„STEINVORHANG" AUS „EINZELTEILEN ~ 60-70CM BREIT UND CA. 2M HOCH / JE NACH KÜCHENWAND
• EXHIBITION

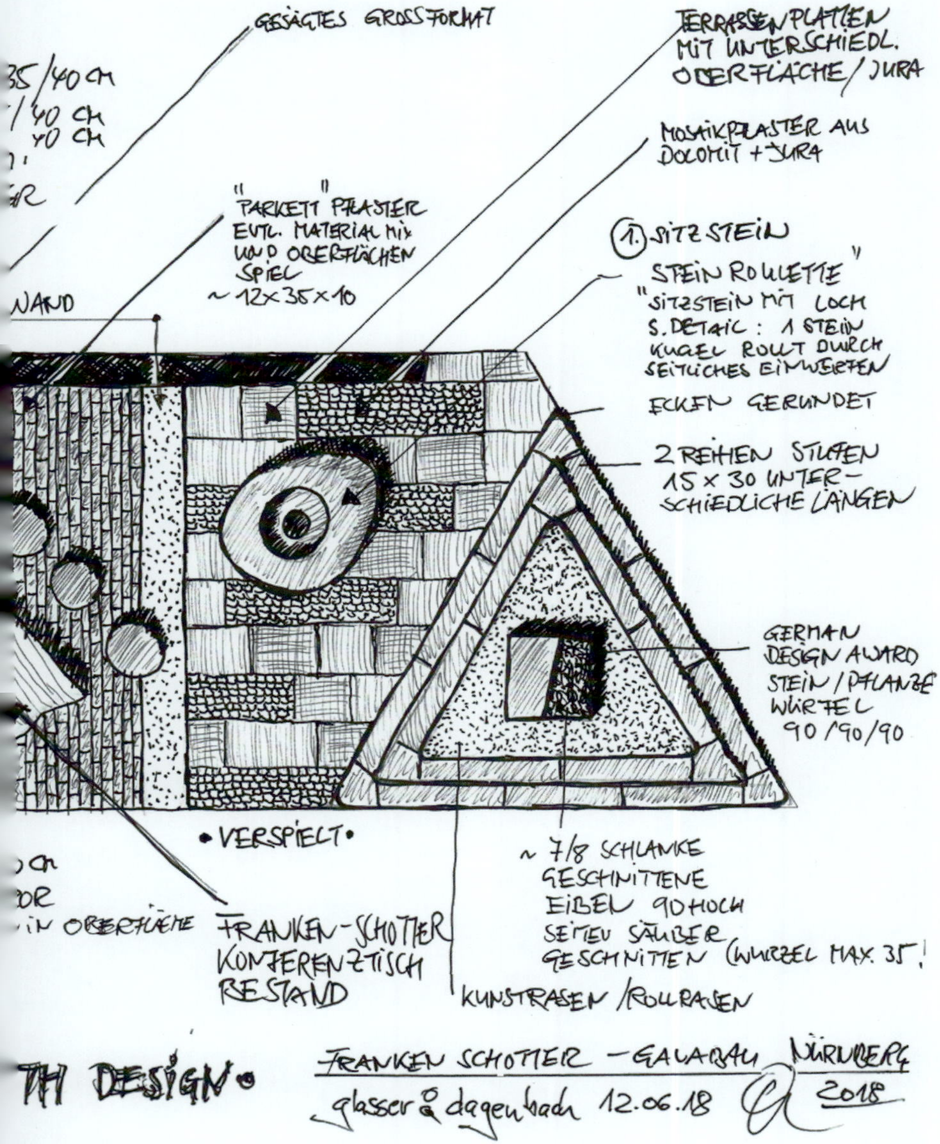

40.A
Realized booth design
Detail of sitting stones and undulating stone wall
2018

40
Exhibition Booth Design
2018

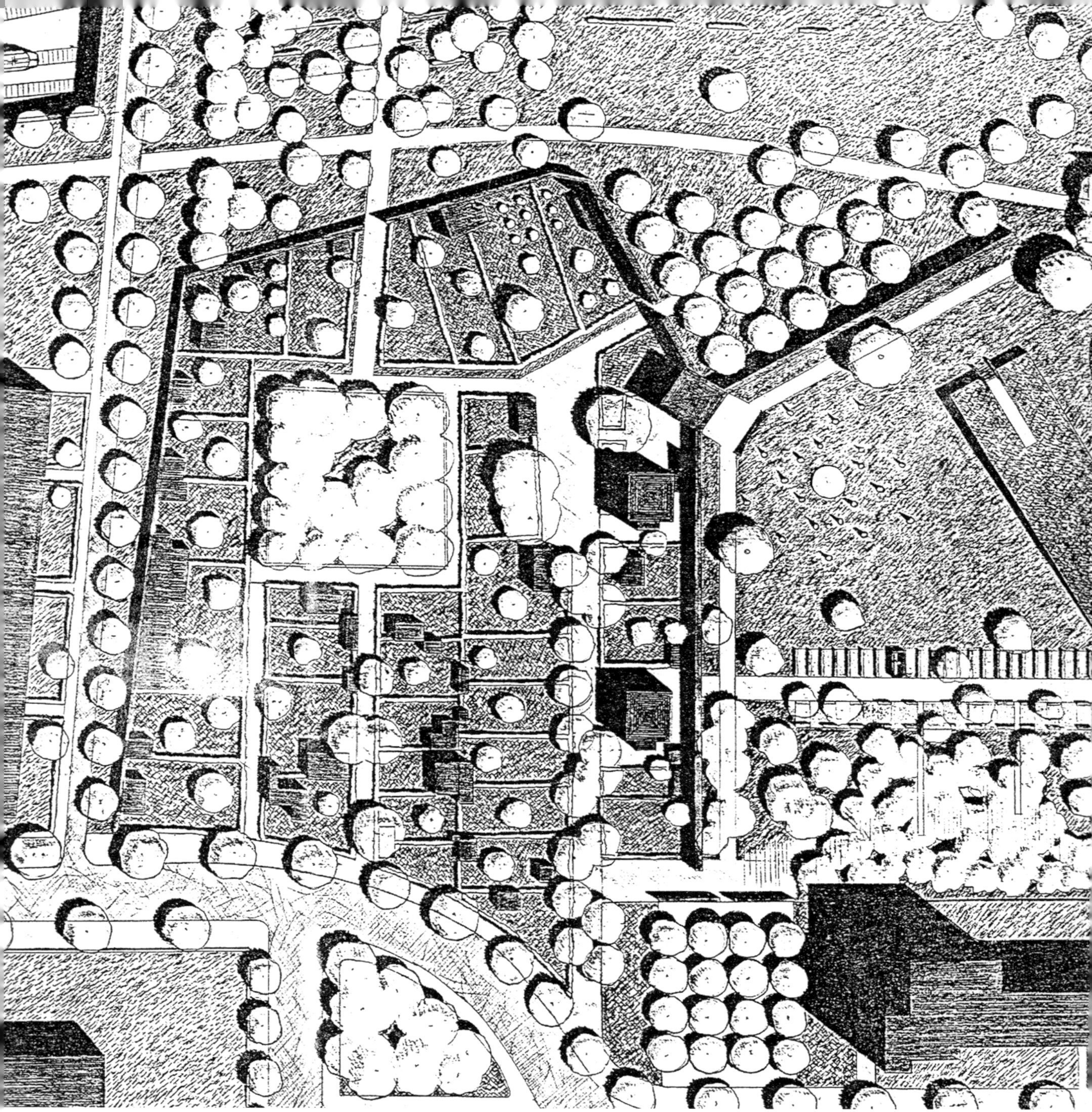

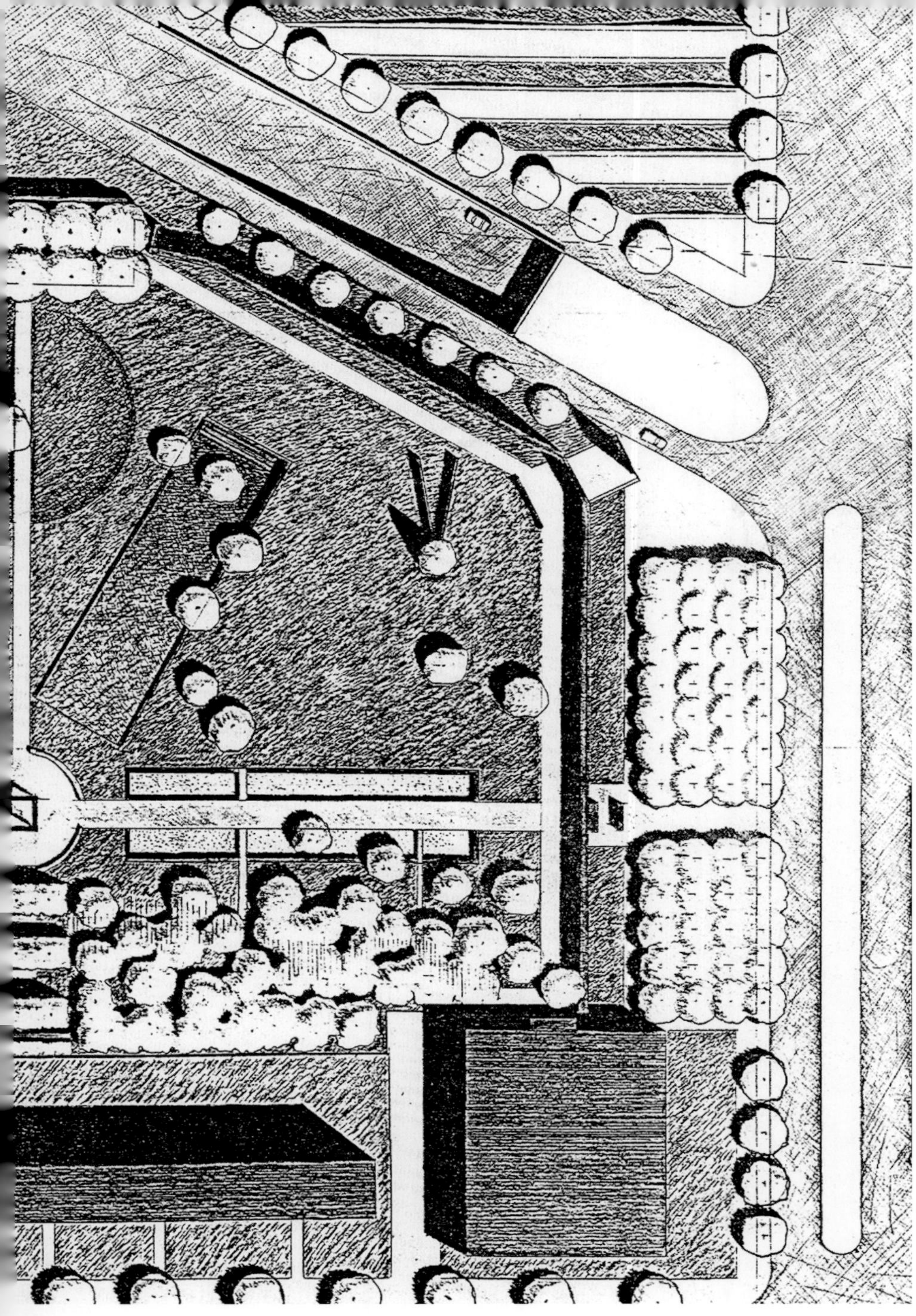

41
History Park
Former Prison Moabit
1993–2006

41.1
Overall plan
of the complex

41.A
Photograph of the central architectural element, close-up view
2006

41.2–4
Several sketches of the central architectural element, the wall passage, and the design of the lock of the park gate

41.B
Photograph of the central architectural element, overall view
2006

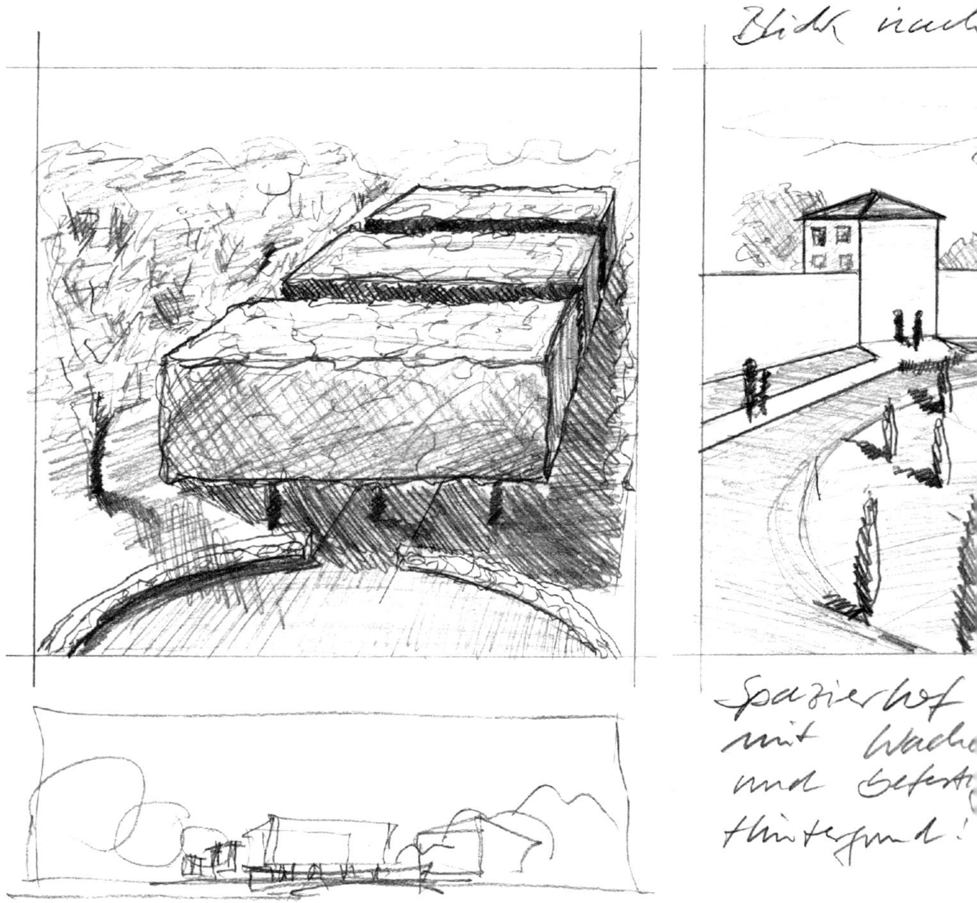

41.5
Two-part sketch of ideas for an area with shaped trees

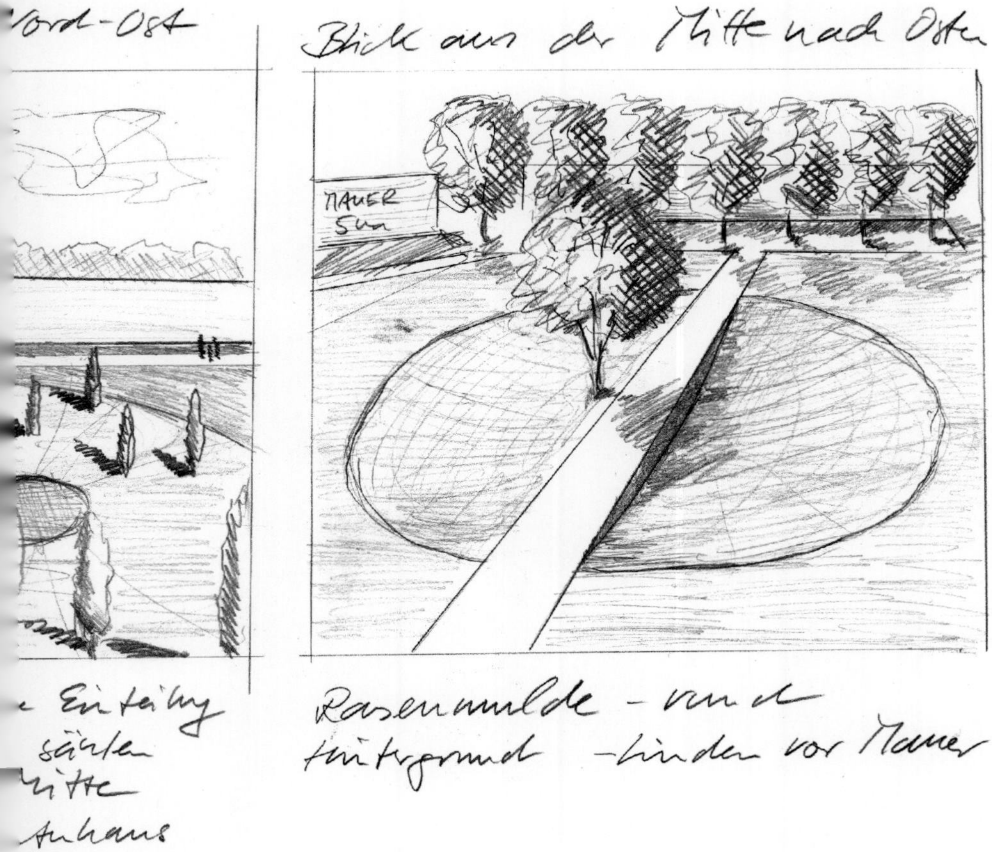

41.6–7
Annotated illustrations: courtyard for walks and lowered grass area

41.C
Detail of the
lowered grass area
2006

41.8
Annotated illustration:
walls

41.D and E
Outside and inside view of the wall passage
2006

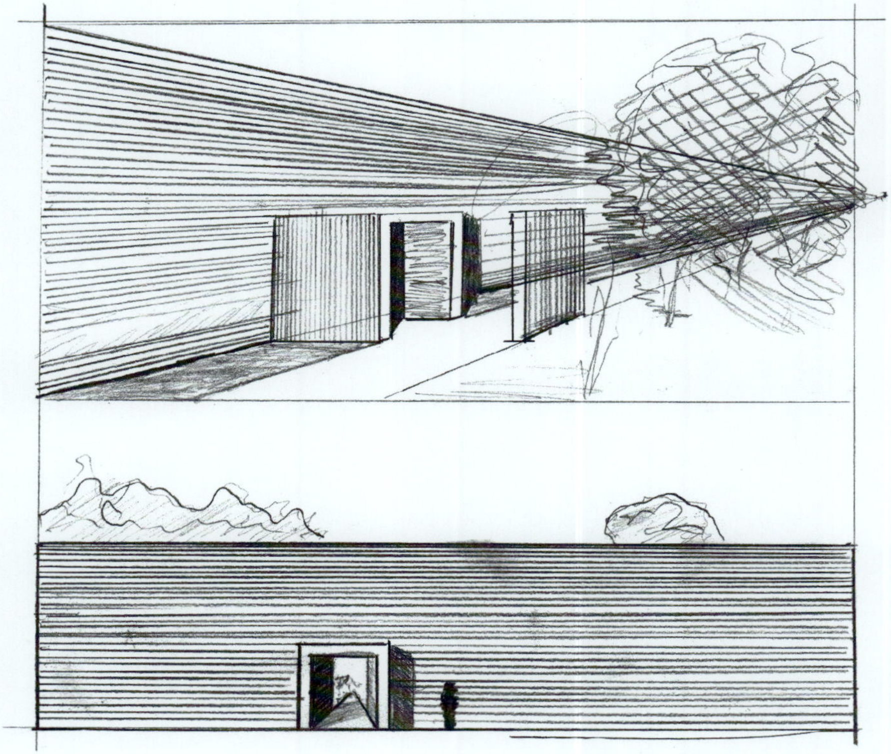

41.9
Two-part illustration: wall passage, outside and inside view

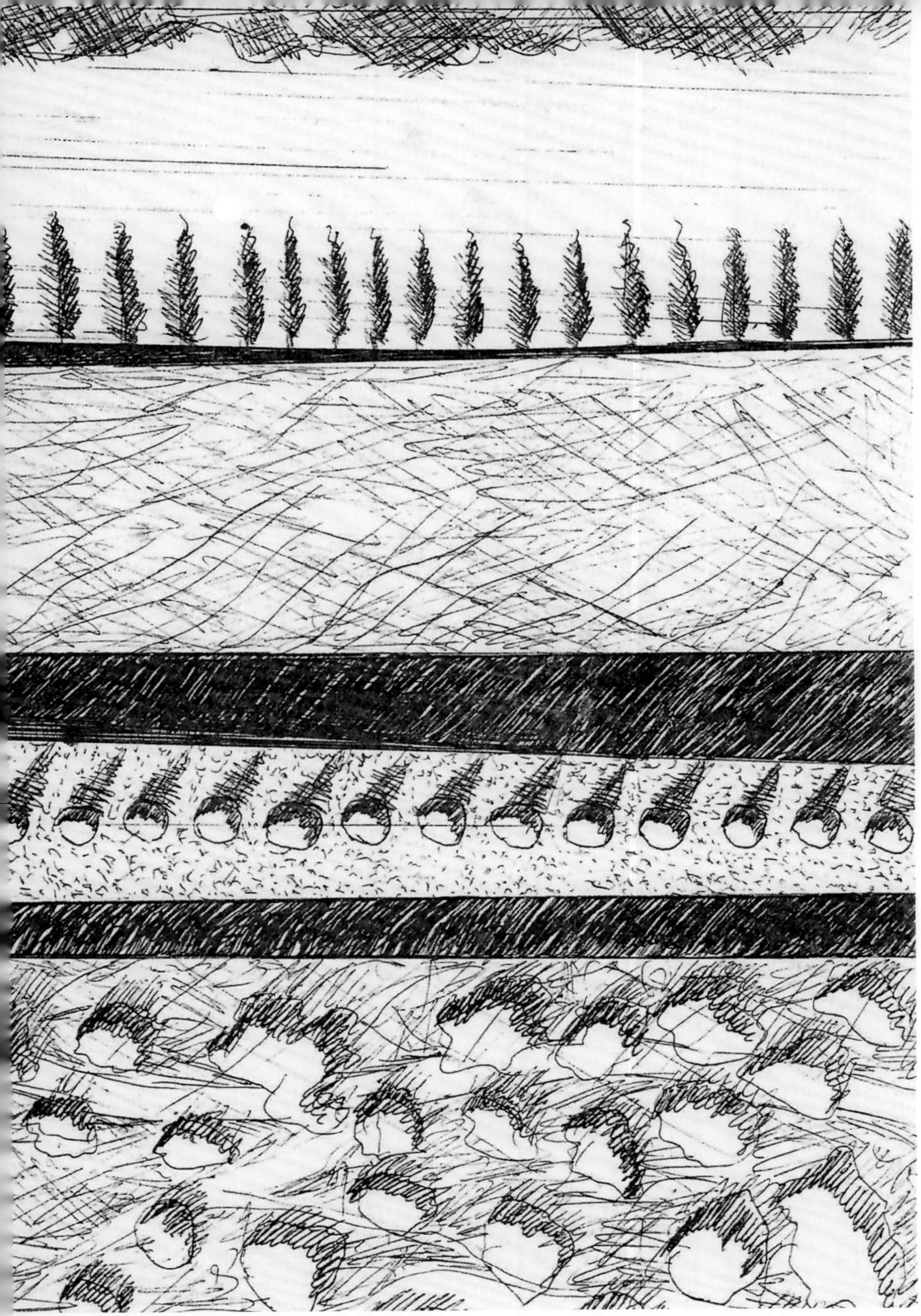

42
Land Art Design
for a Former Runway
1997

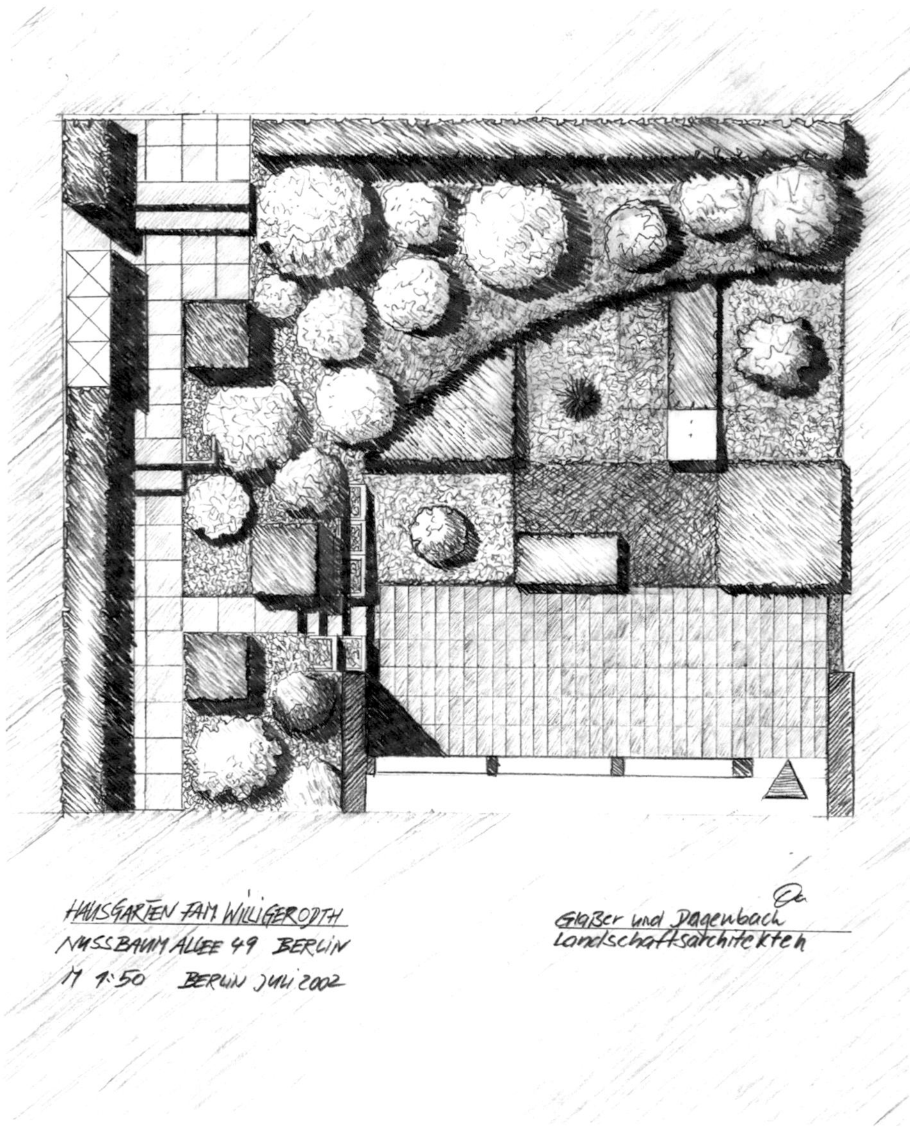

43
Mathematical
Private Garden
2002

43.B
Photograph: part of the garden with a sculpture by Elgin Willigerodt, 2000

43.A
Rendering: site plan, design variant

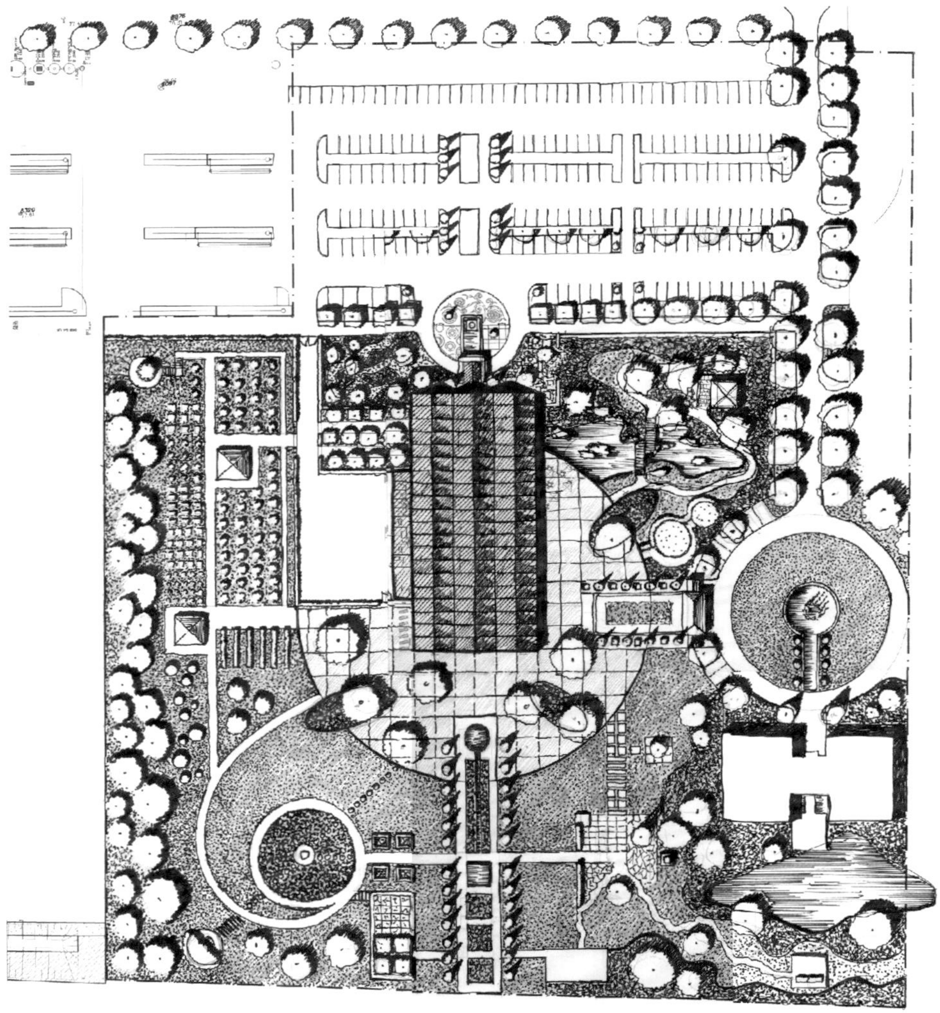

44
Garten von Ehren
2006

44.1
General plan of the entrance area in front of the new garden center

44.A
Aerial photograph of baroque garden © Arndt Haug 2006

44.2
Plan view drawing of the area at the rear of the centre, with different designs and a water basin

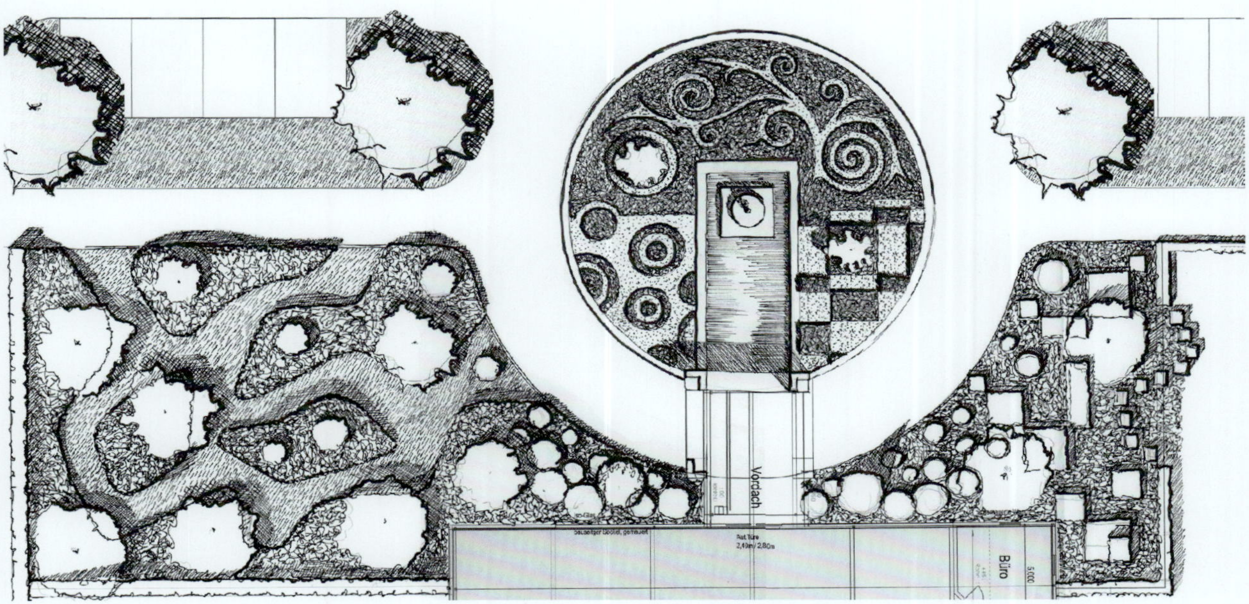

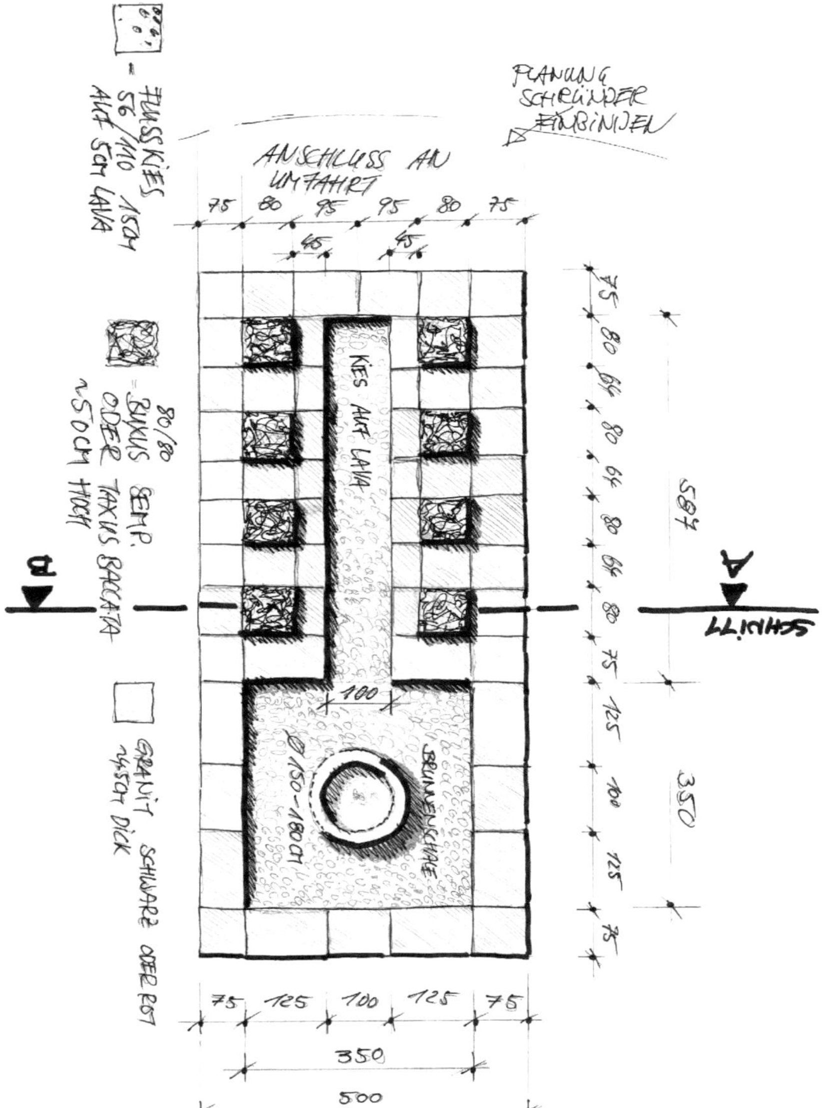

44.3
Technical design drawing of the front water basin, with dimensional and material specifications

44.B
Detail of the fountain bowl in the front water basin
2006

44.C and D
Photographs of the quadrant segments
2006

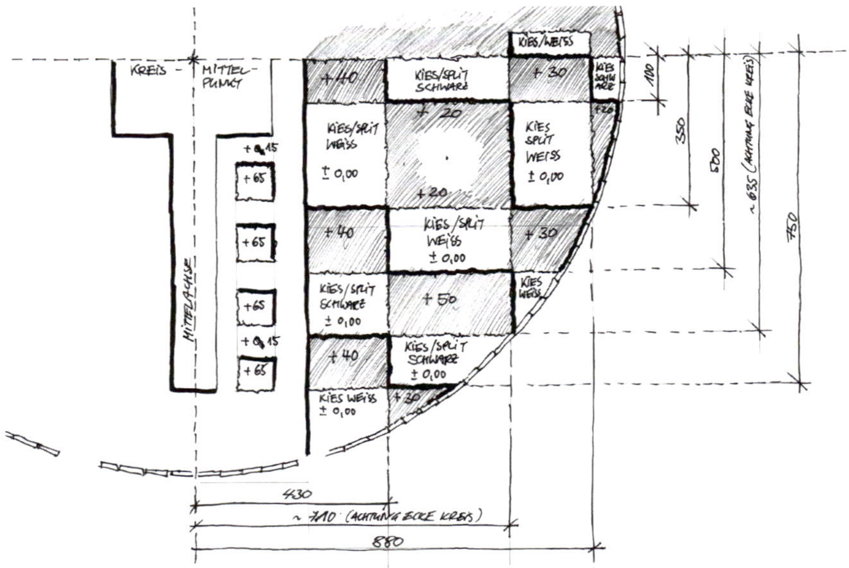

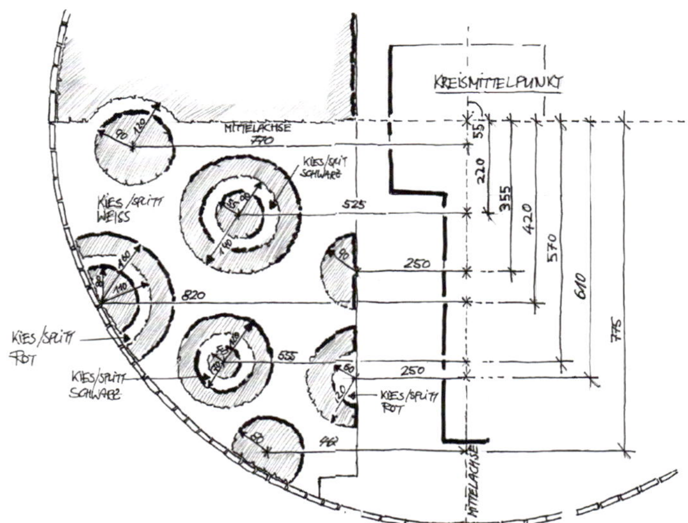

44.4 and 5
Two technical drawings of quadrant segments, with cubic and circular plant-gravel sections

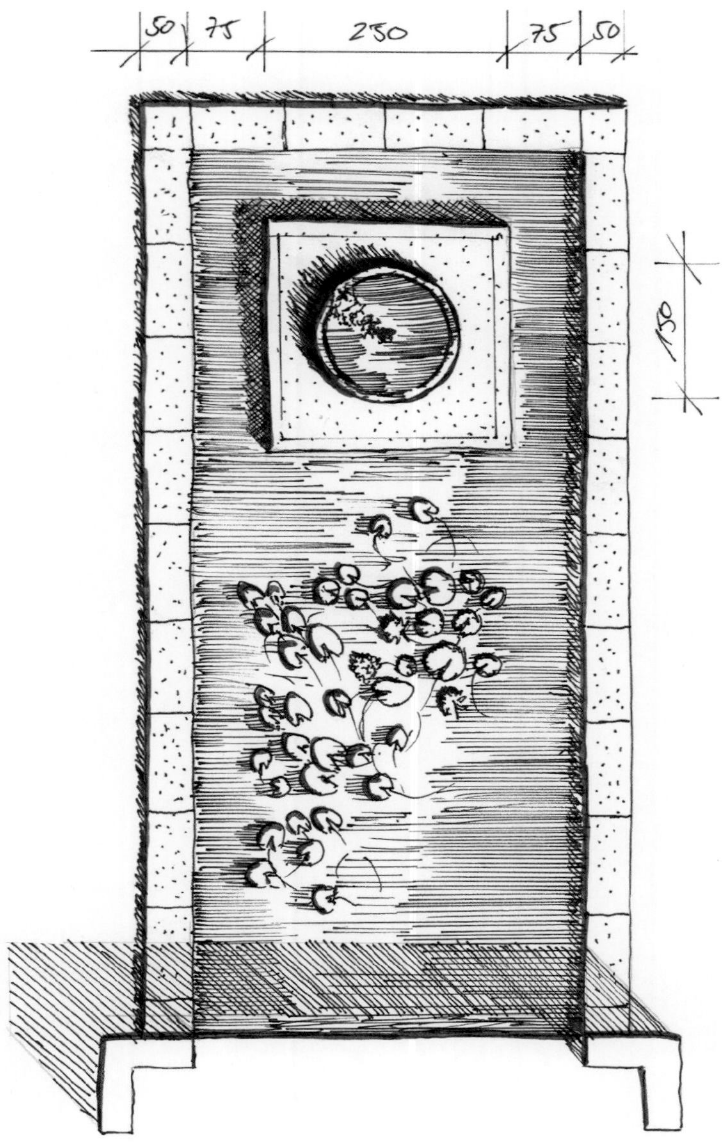

44.6
Design drawing with dimensional data for the rear water basin

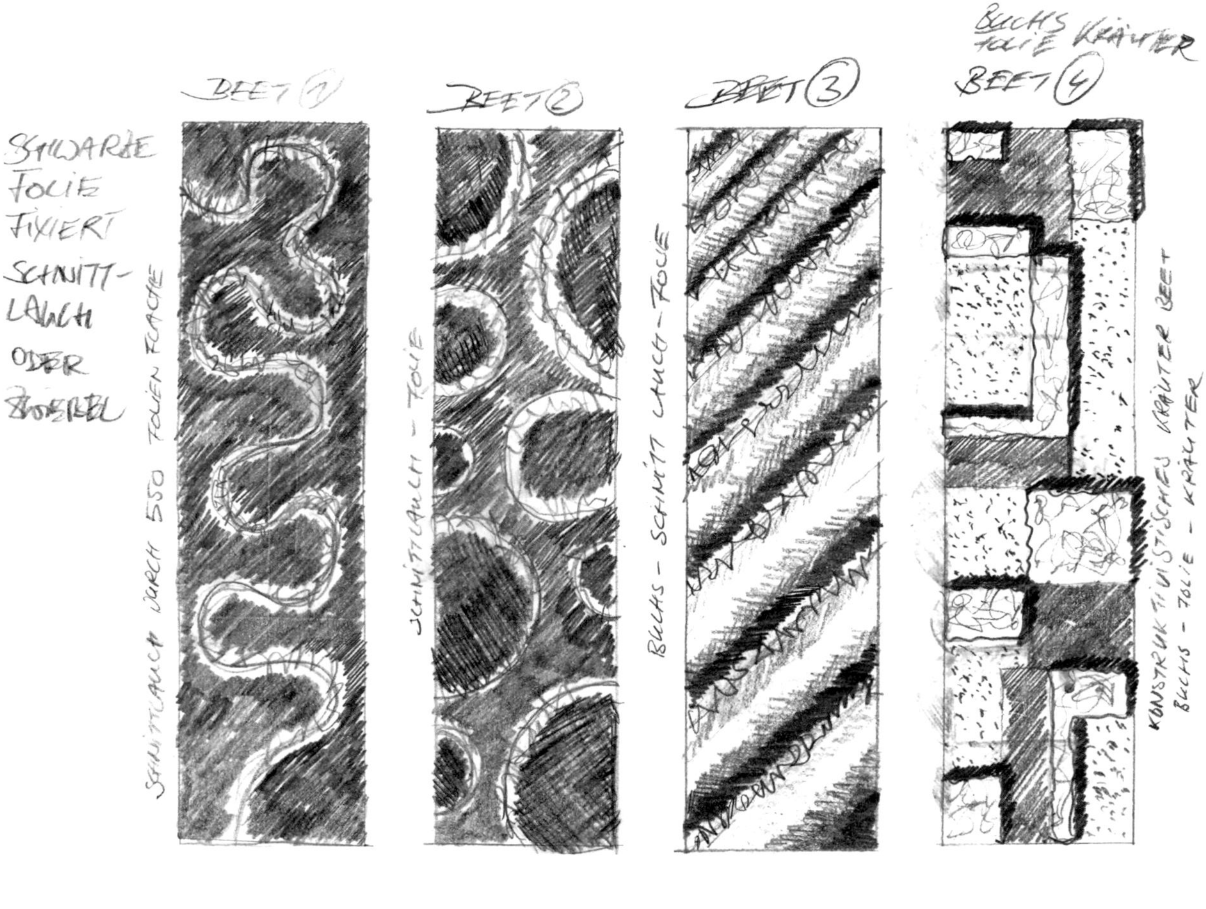
BUCHS
FOLIE KRÄUTER
BEET 1
BEET 2
BEET 3
BEET 4
SCHWARZE
FOLIE
FIXIERT
SCHNITT-
LAUCH
ODER
SCHNITTLAUCH - FOLIE
BUCHS - SCHNITTLAUCH - FOLIE
BUCHS - FOLIE - KRÄUTER

45.A
Photograph: top view
2008

45
Garden Art Installation
G'Mies Bed 2008

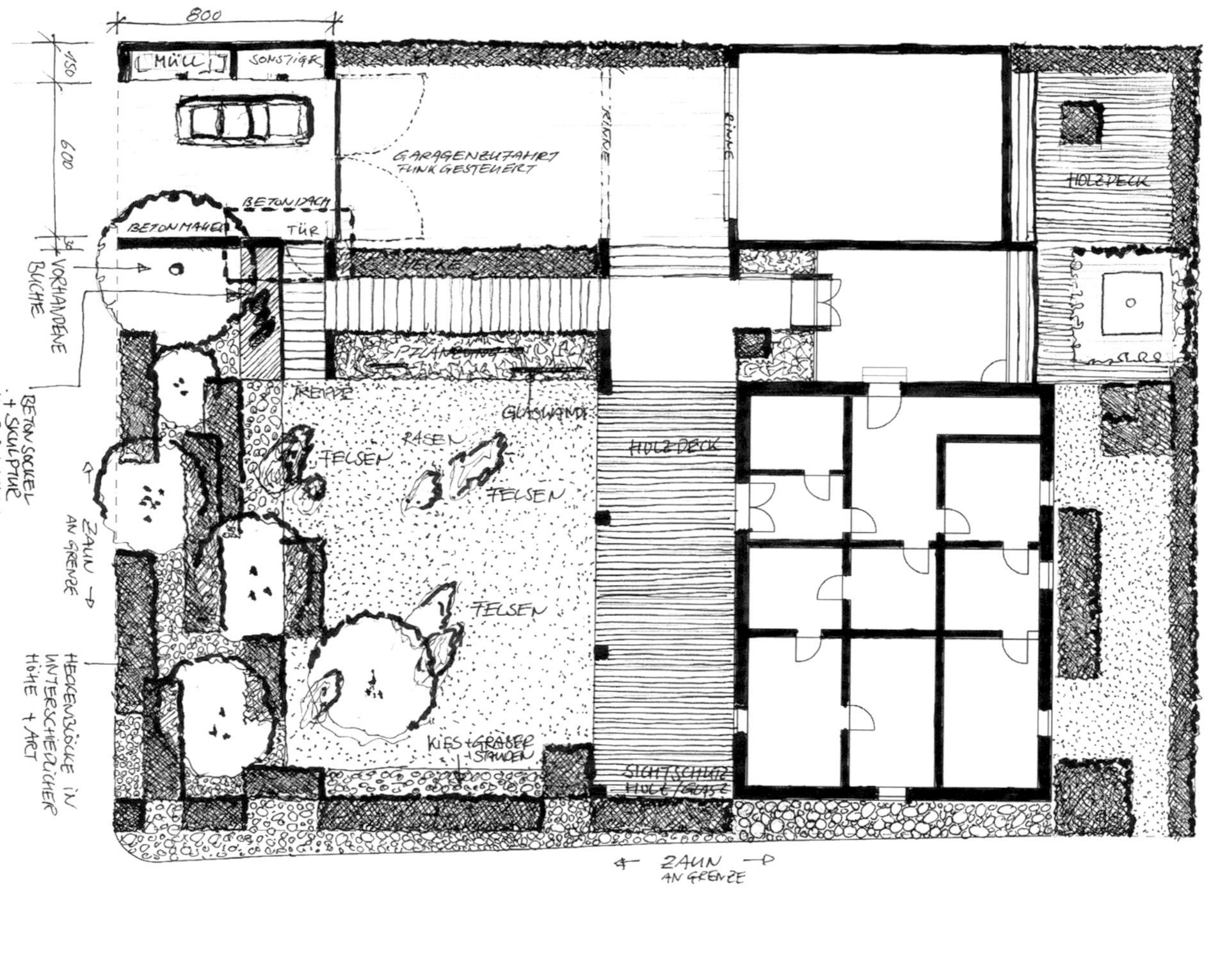
800
150
600
MÜLL
SONSTIGES
GARAGENZUFAHRT
FUNK GESTEUERT
BETONDACH
BETONMAUER
TÜR
RINNE
HOLZDECK
VORHANDENE BUCHE
BETONSOCKEL + SKULPTUR IN BLICKACHSE EINGANG
PFLANZUNG
TREPPE
GLASWAND
RASEN
FELSEN
FELSEN
FELSEN
HOLZDECK
ZAUN AN GRENZE
HECKENBLÖCKE IN UNTERSCHIEDLICHER HÖHE + ART
KIES + GRÄSER + STAUDEN
SICHTSCHUTZ HOLZ/GLAS
ZAUN AN GRENZE

46.1 and 2
Private Garden
2008

47.A
Photograph: detail
2011

47.B
Photograph: outside view of the wall
2011

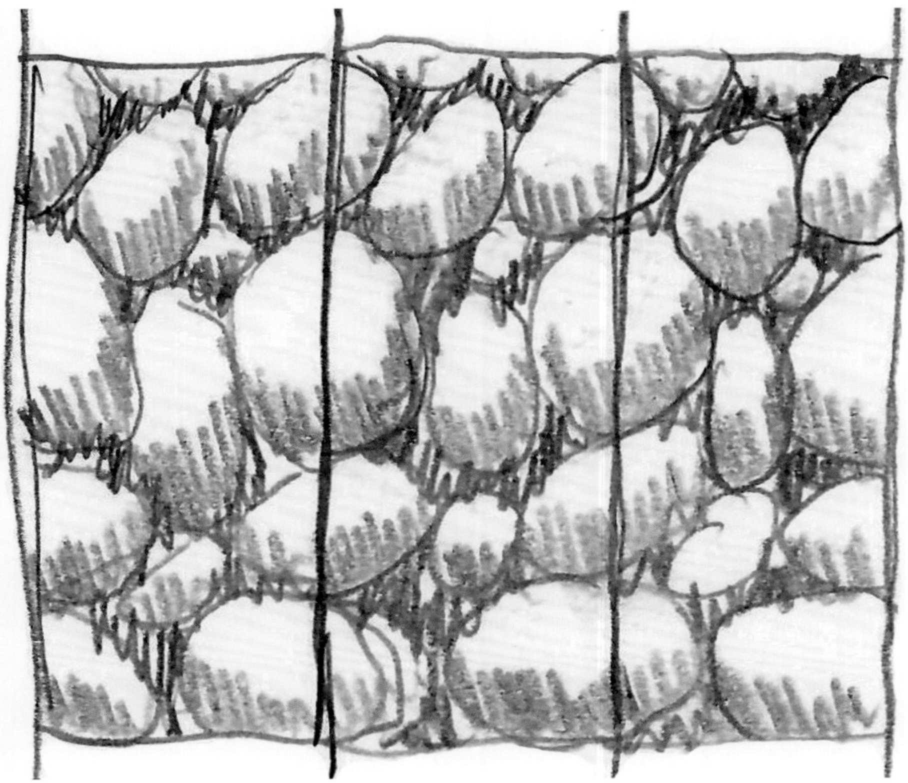

47.1 and 2
Oval Briquette Wall
2009

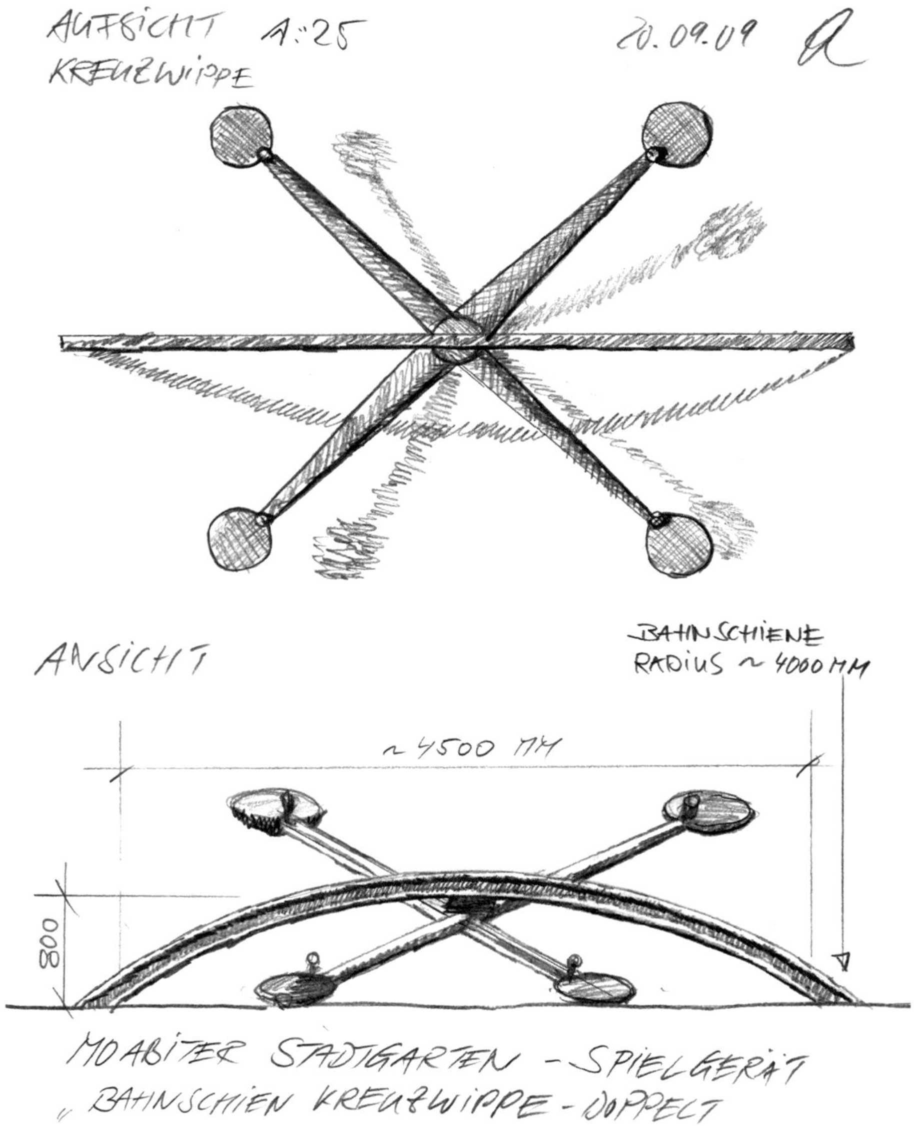

48
Seesaw, Swing, and Hammock: Play Equipment made of Railway Tracks
2009

48.1
View and top view: cruciform twin-seesaw made of railway tracks

48.A
Photograph of the partner swing
2012

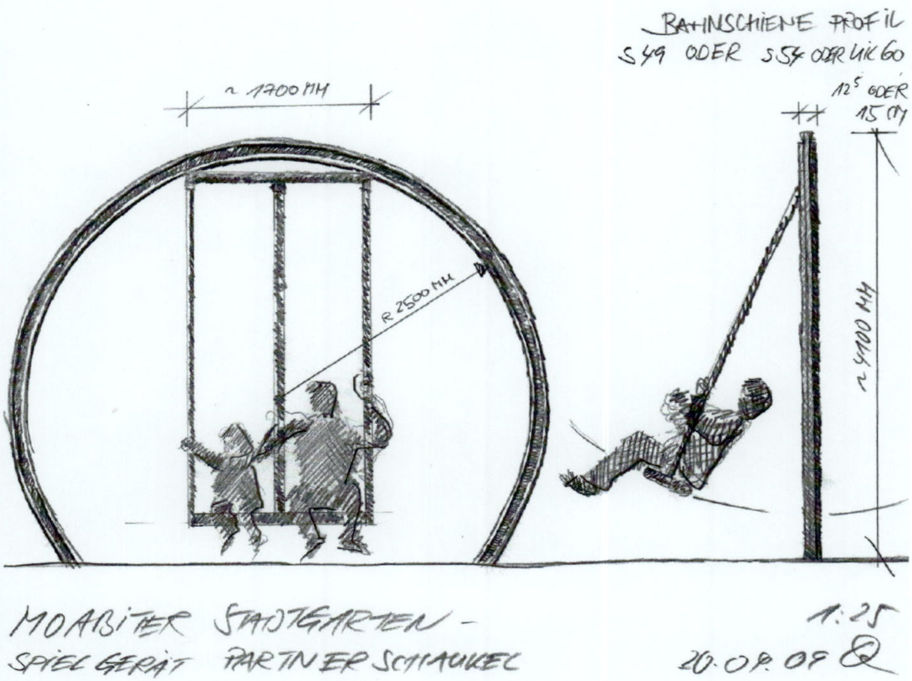

48.2
Partner Swing:
front and side view

48.B
Photograph of the
hammock
2012

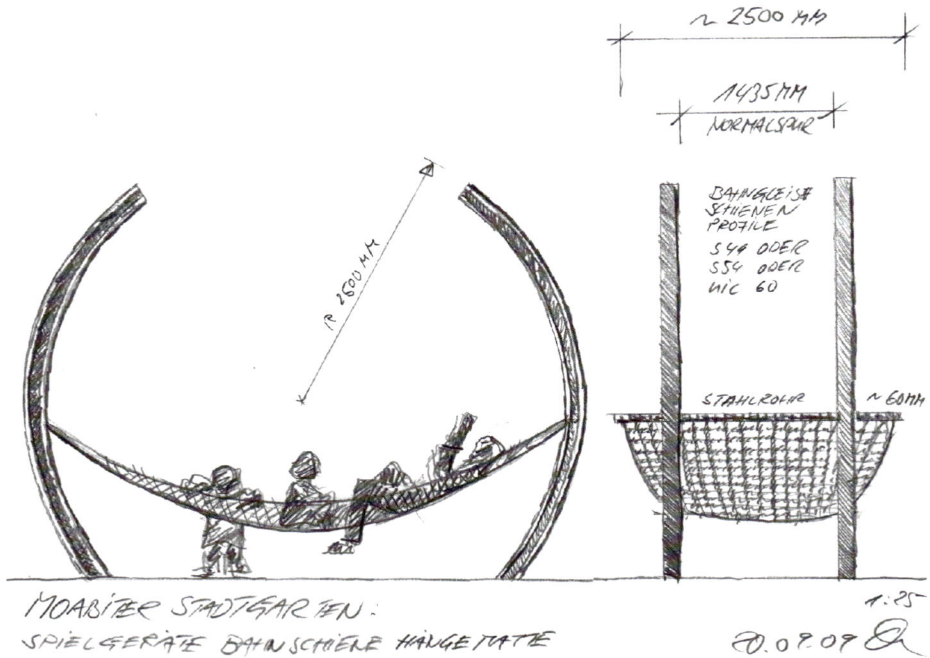

48.3
Hammock:
front and side view

48.4
Annotated illustration with swing and seesaw, to the right the hammock

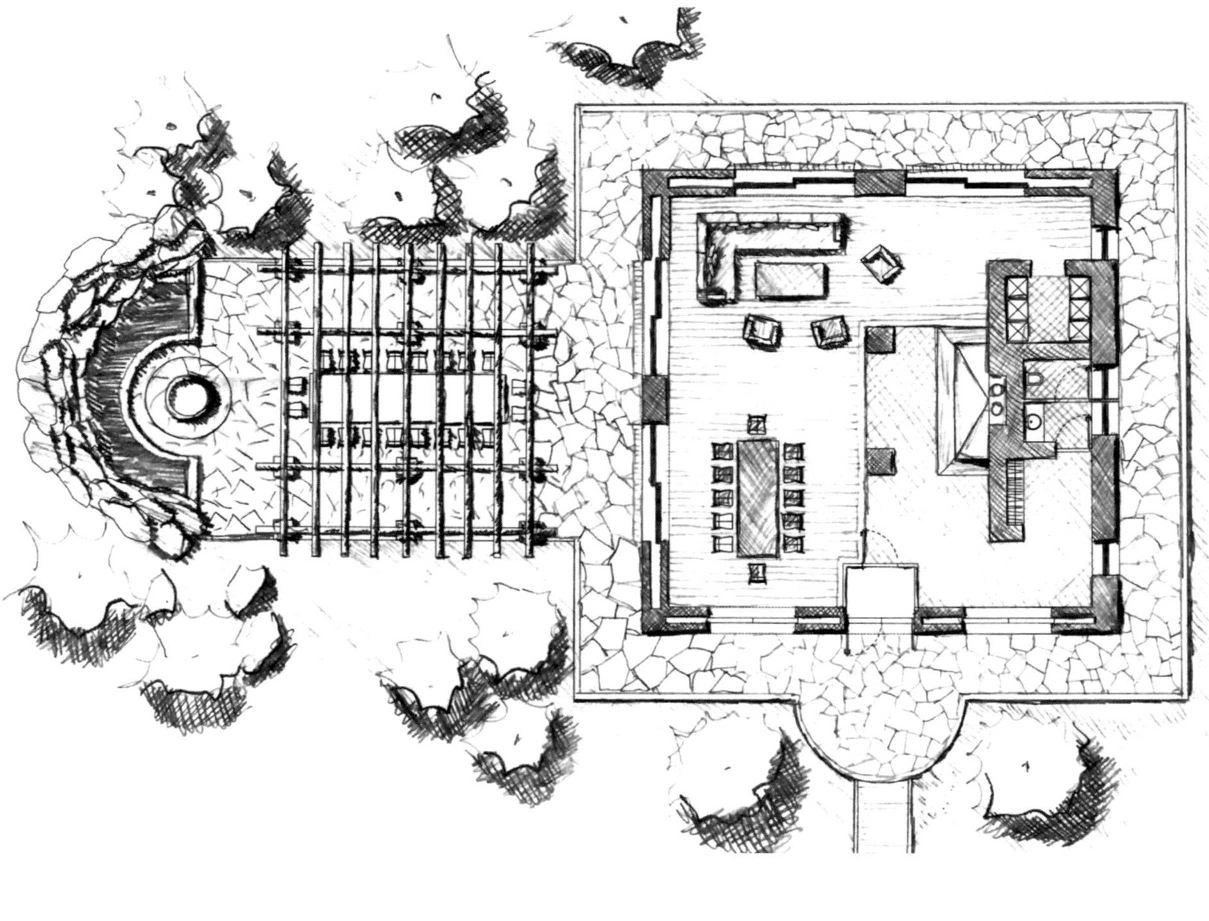

49.1 and 2
Barbecue area
in Alpine style
and Pergola Garden
2009

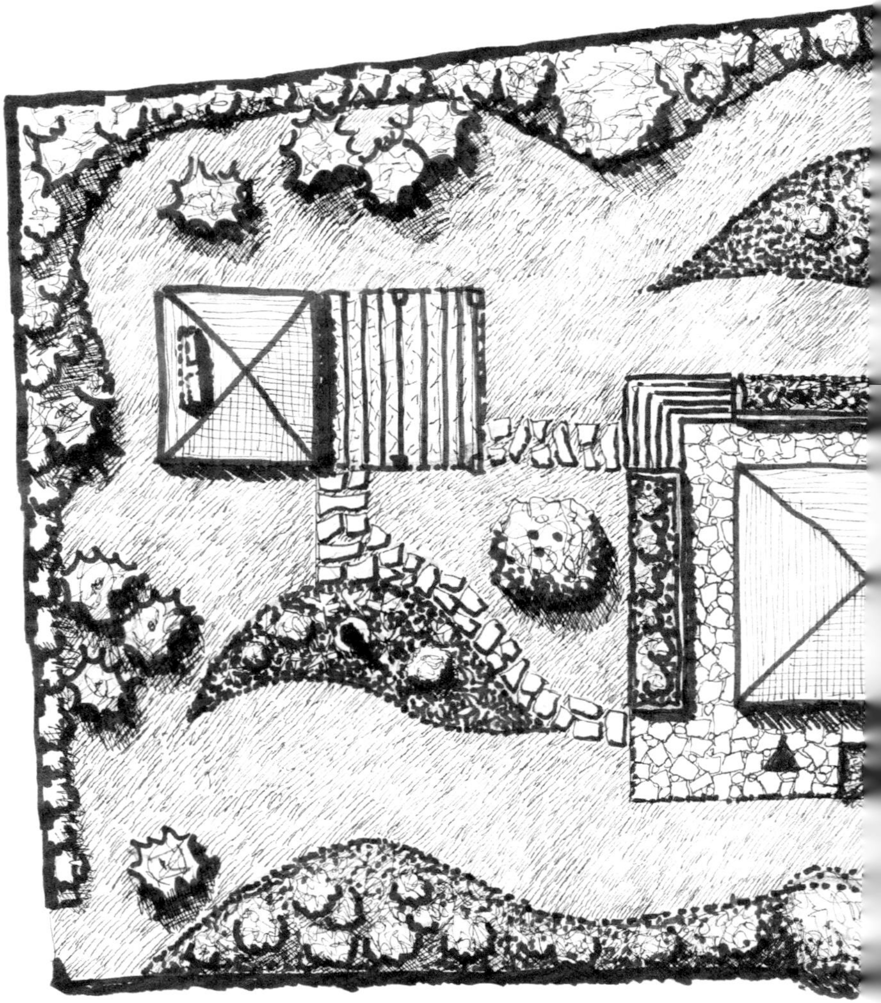

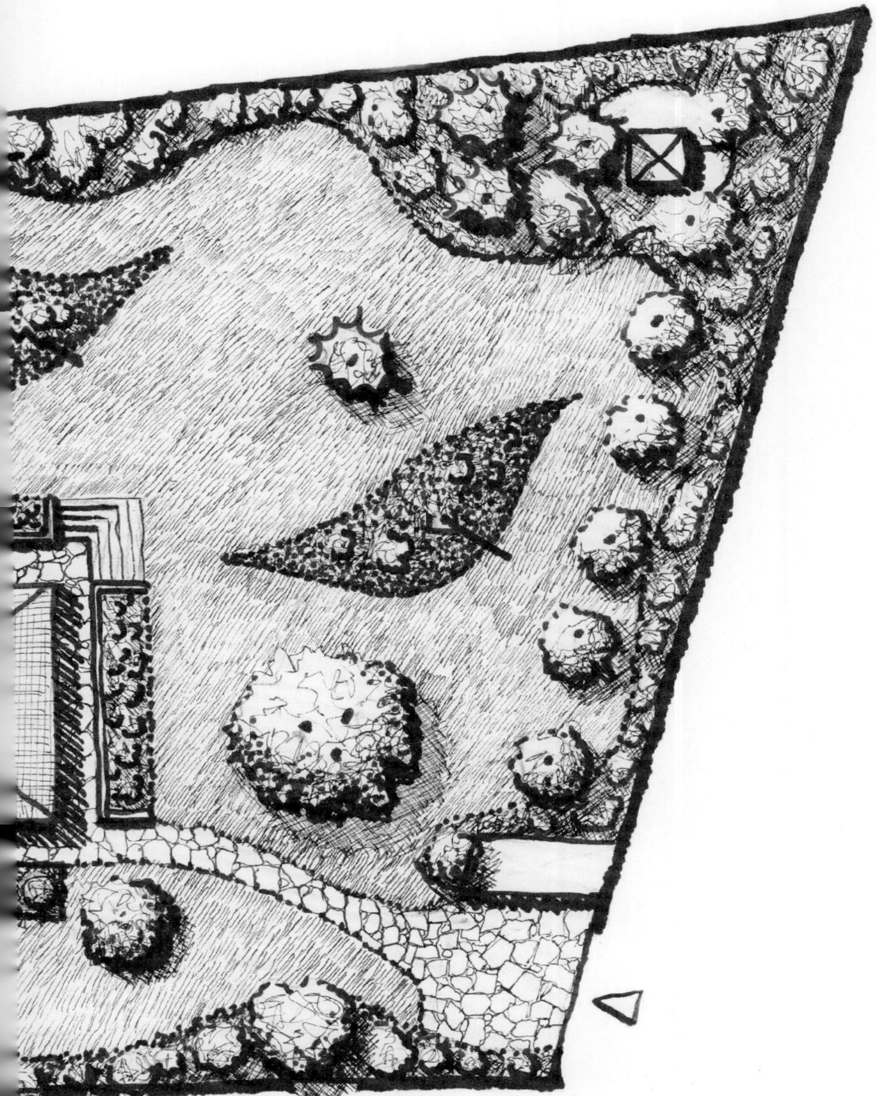

50
Country House Garden
2012

51.A
Photograph: front garden
2015

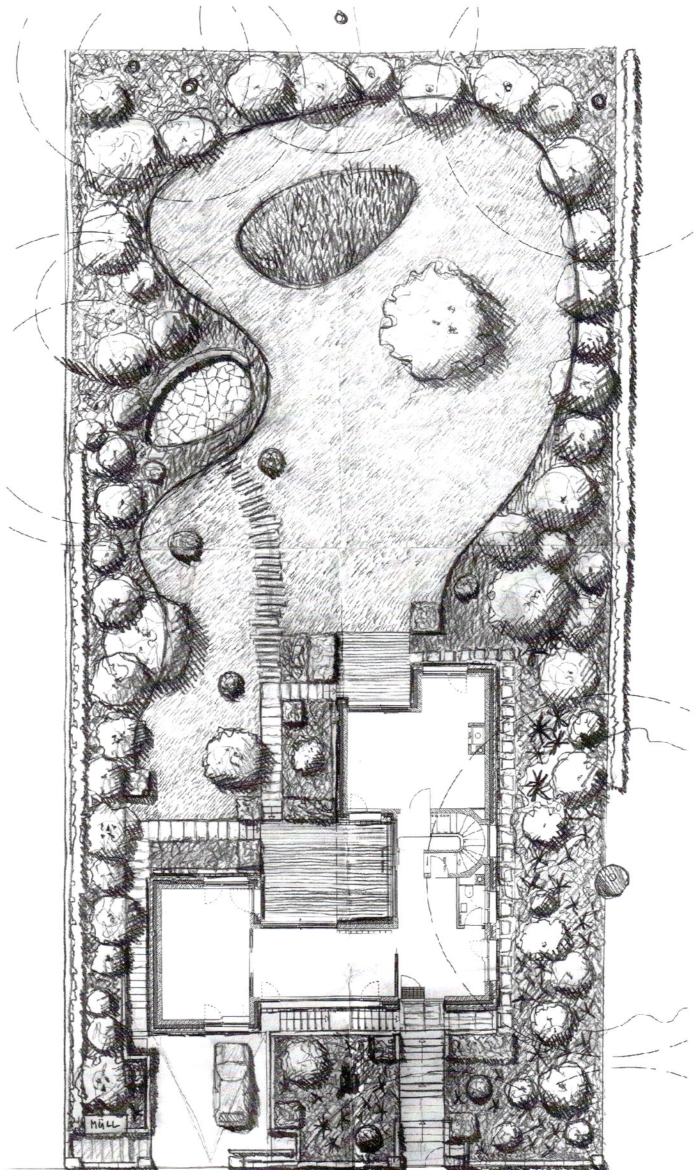

51
Private Garden for a
Bauhaus-style house
2015

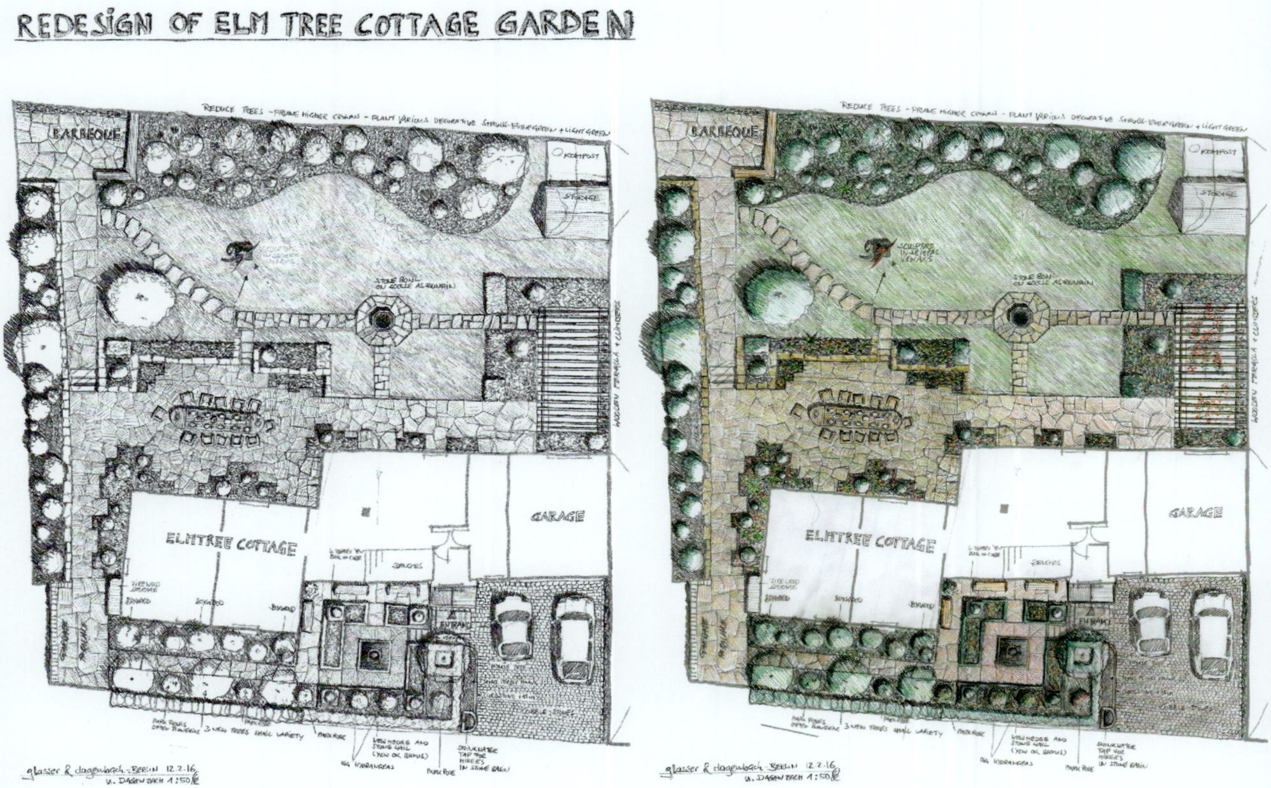

52.1 and 2
Redesign of
Elmtree Cottage Garden
2016

53.A
Rendering

53.B
Rendering:
central glass-steel structure

53
Center
of a Botanical Garden
2016

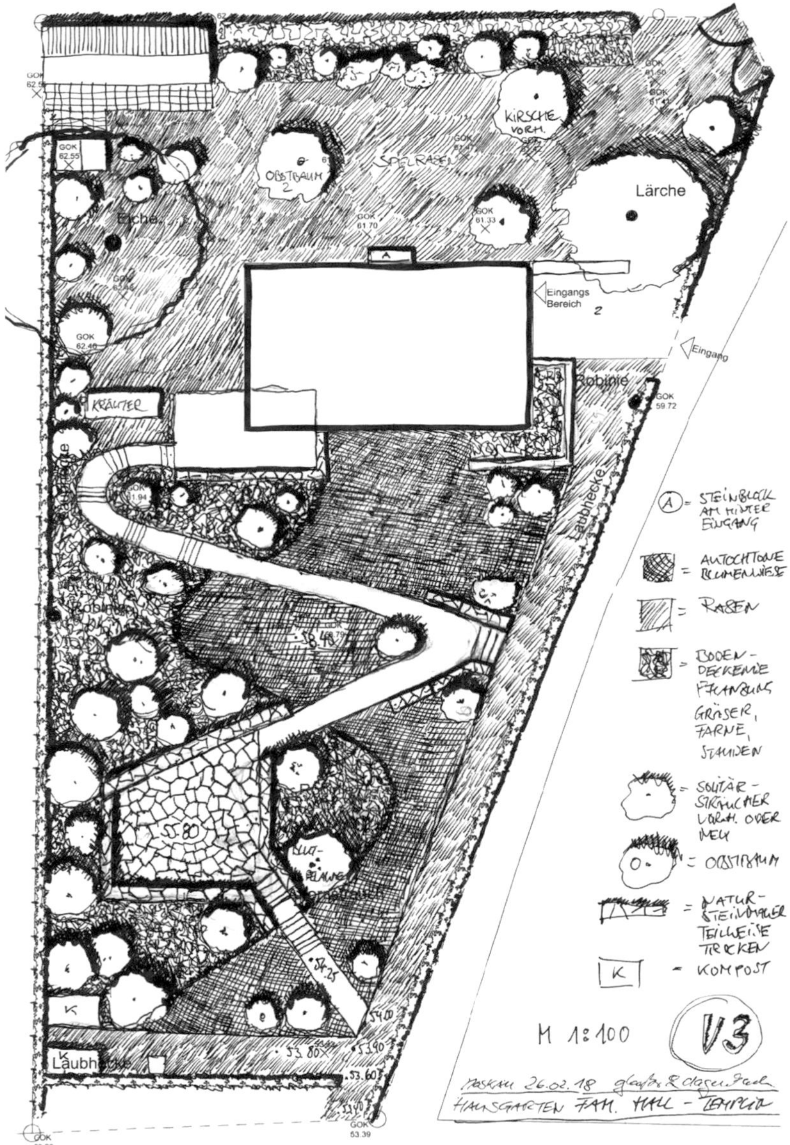

54
Private Garden
2018

MIXED THEMES

Graphic Art

Sculpture

Applied Art

55.1 and 2
Biomorph I and II
1974

Graphic Art

56.1
Garden Views Japan:
Part of the Garden at the
Shoden-ji Temple, Kyoto
1982

56.2
Garden Views Japan:
Part of the Garden at the
Entsu-ji Temple, Kyoto
1982

57
Haniwa and Isolator
1983

58
Portrait of a
Zen Buddhist Priest
1983

Graphic Art

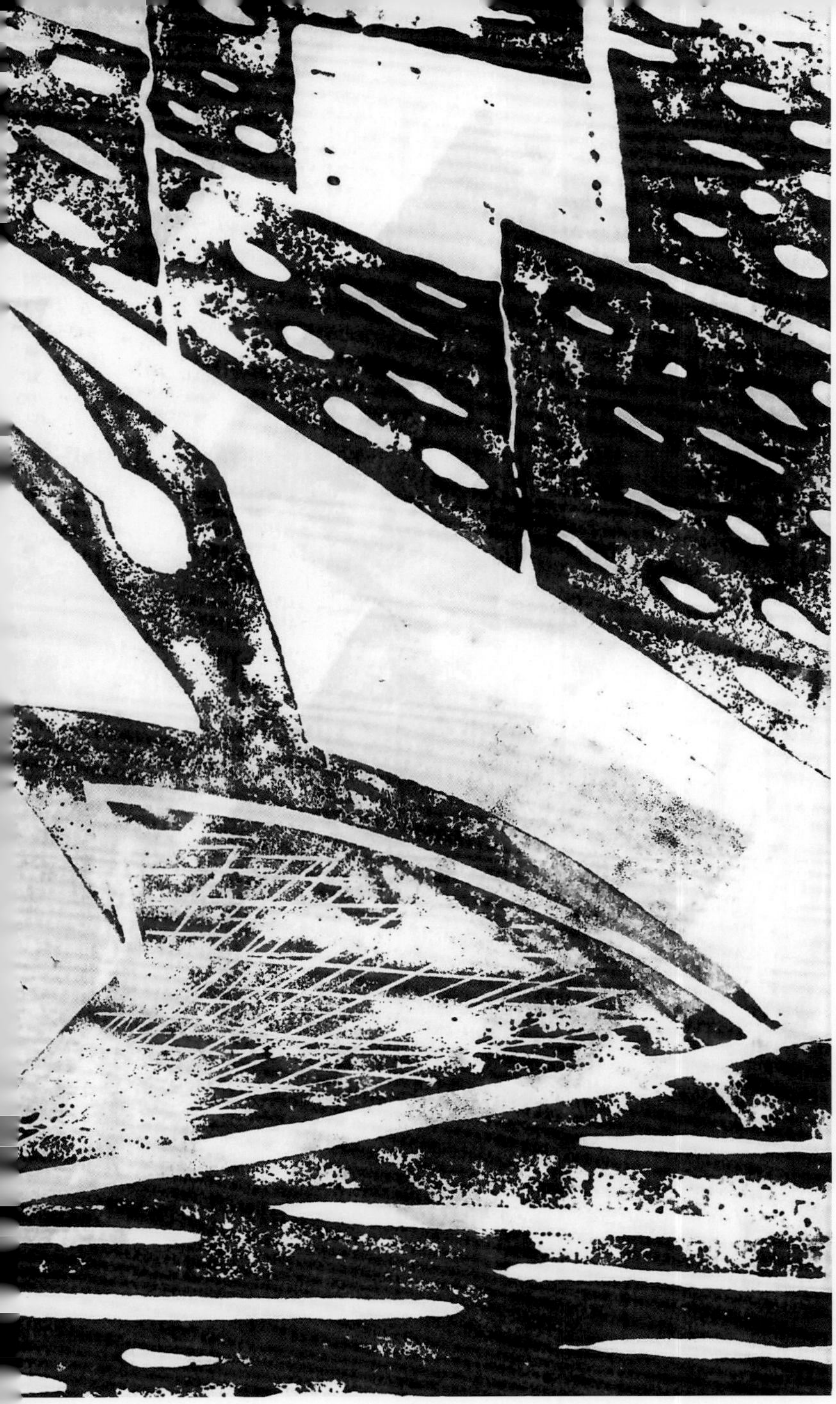

59.1 and 2
Scissors' Ballet
1984

60.1 and 2
Grandma Maria and
Grandpa August
1985 and 1986

61.1
Rocks in Norway:
Coastline in southern
Norway close to Larvik
1986

61.2
Rocks in Norway:
Labradorite quarry in
southern Norway
1986

62.1
Sketch for Kids:
Fish and Balloon
1992

62.2
Sketch for Kids:
Fish
1992

62.3
Sketch for Kids:
Elephant Couple
1992

63.1–3
Turtle Sketch
and Snail Shell Sketches
2016

64.1–6
Yucca Sketches
2017

65.1–3
Juniper Sketches
2017

66
'Square Head' Standing on its Feet, on its Head, and Kneeling
1983

66.A–C
Photographs of the sculpture
in two different positions

67.A–C
Photographs of the sculpture, front and side views
1984

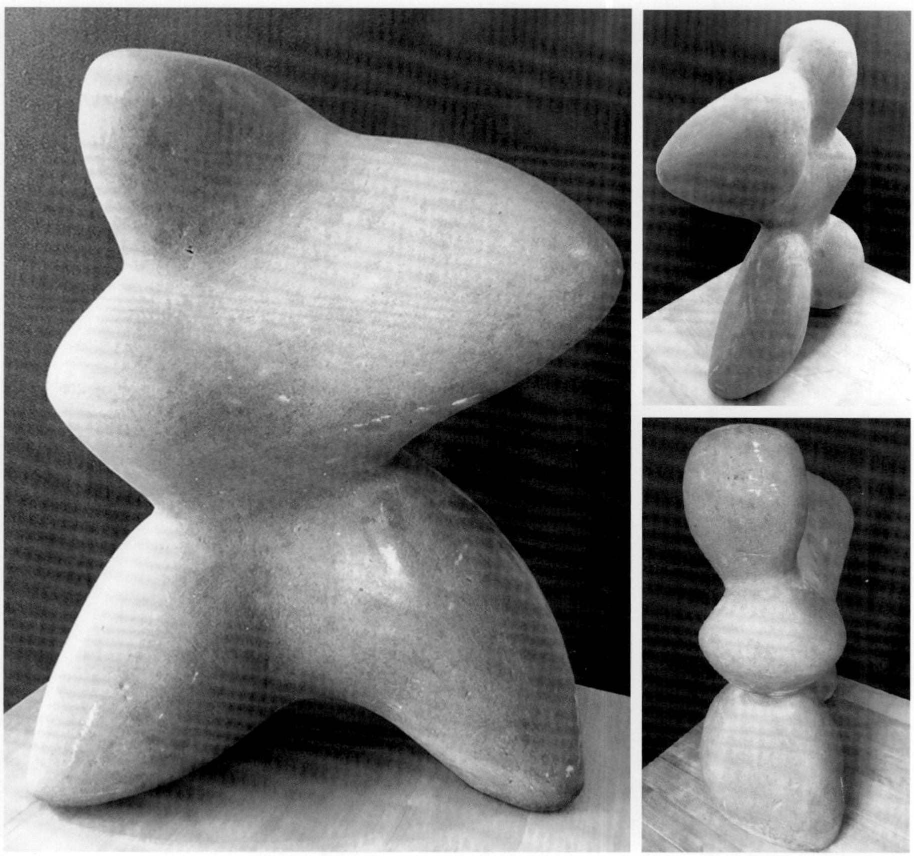

67
Torso
1984

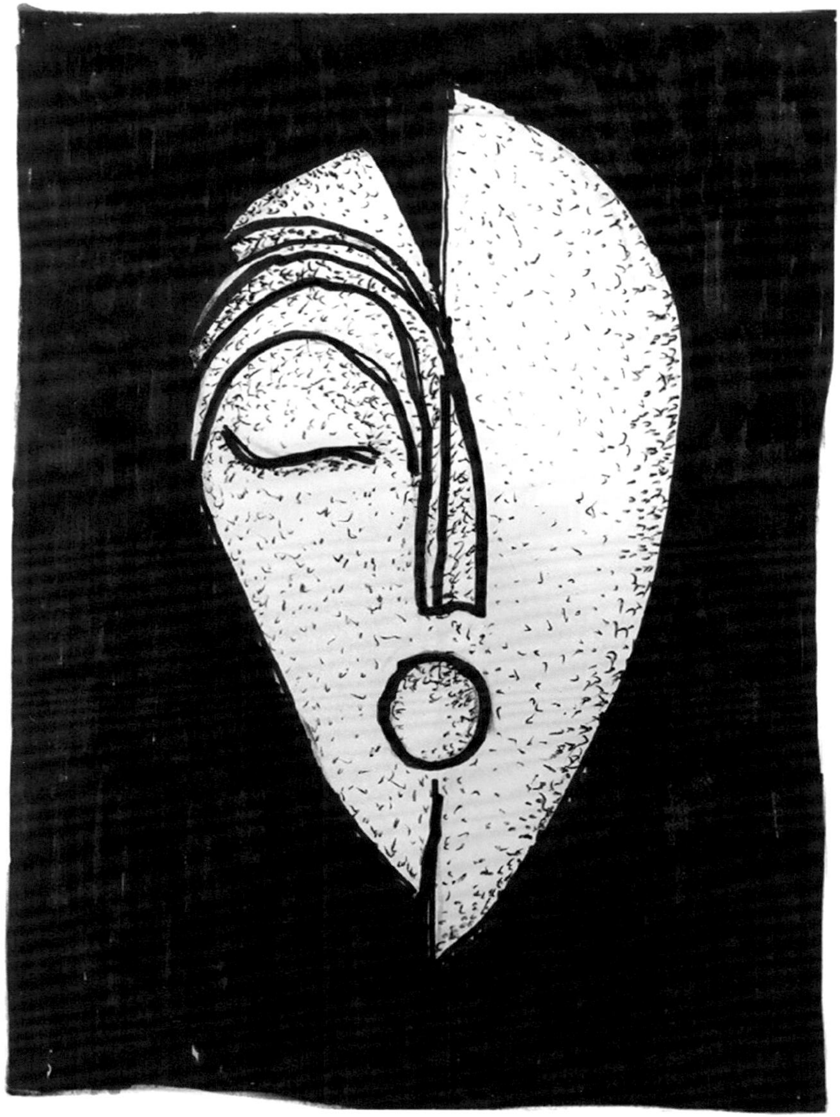

68
Golden Mask
1985

68.A and B
Photographs:
front view and detail
2018

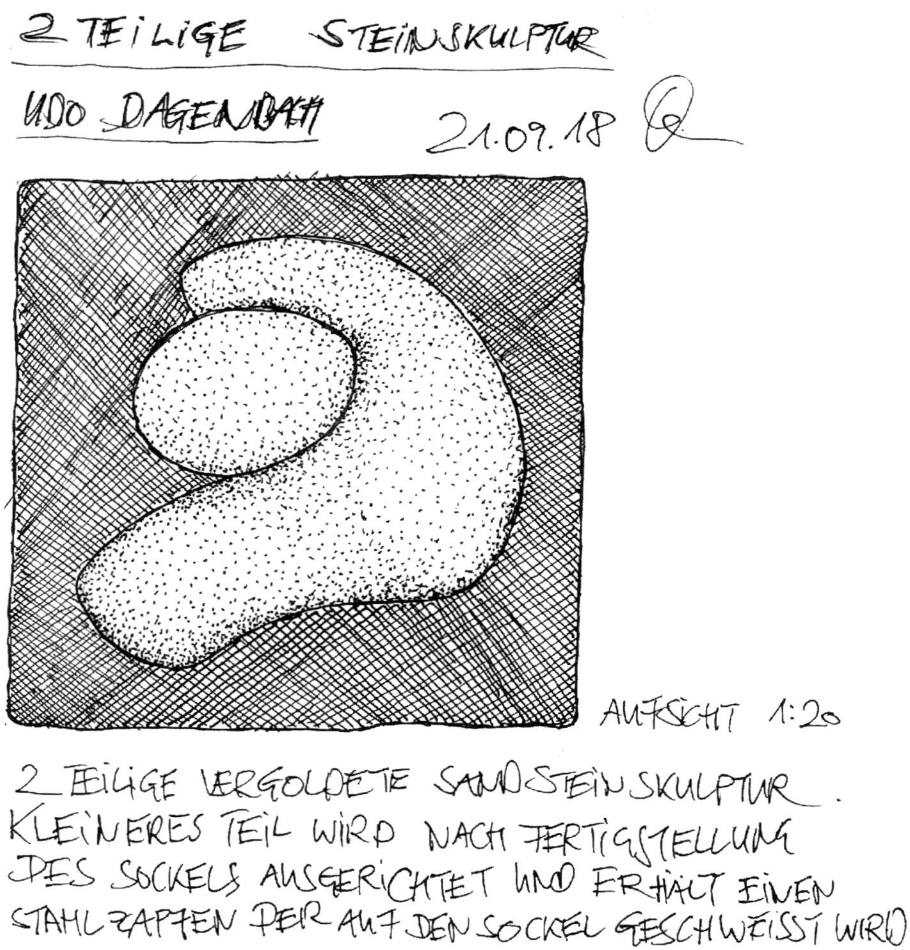
2 TEILIGE STEINSKULPTUR
UDO DAGENBACH
21.09.18
AUFSICHT 1:20
2 TEILIGE VERGOLDETE SANDSTEINSKULPTUR.
KLEINERES TEIL WIRD NACH FERTIGSTELLUNG
DES SOCKELS AUSGERICHTET UND ERHÄLT EINEN
STAHLZAPFEN DER AUF DEN SOCKEL GESCHWEISST WIRD

69.A and B
Photographs of the two-piece, gold-plated sculpture on its new pedestal, 2018

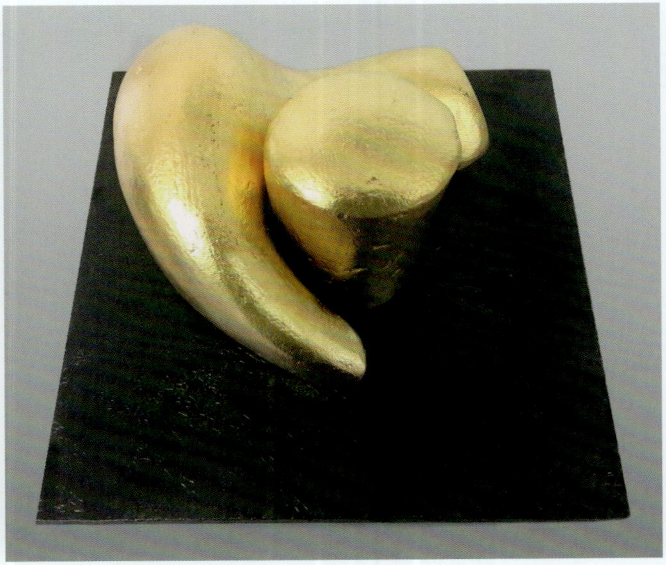

69
Two-piece
Stone Sculpture
Embedded
2018

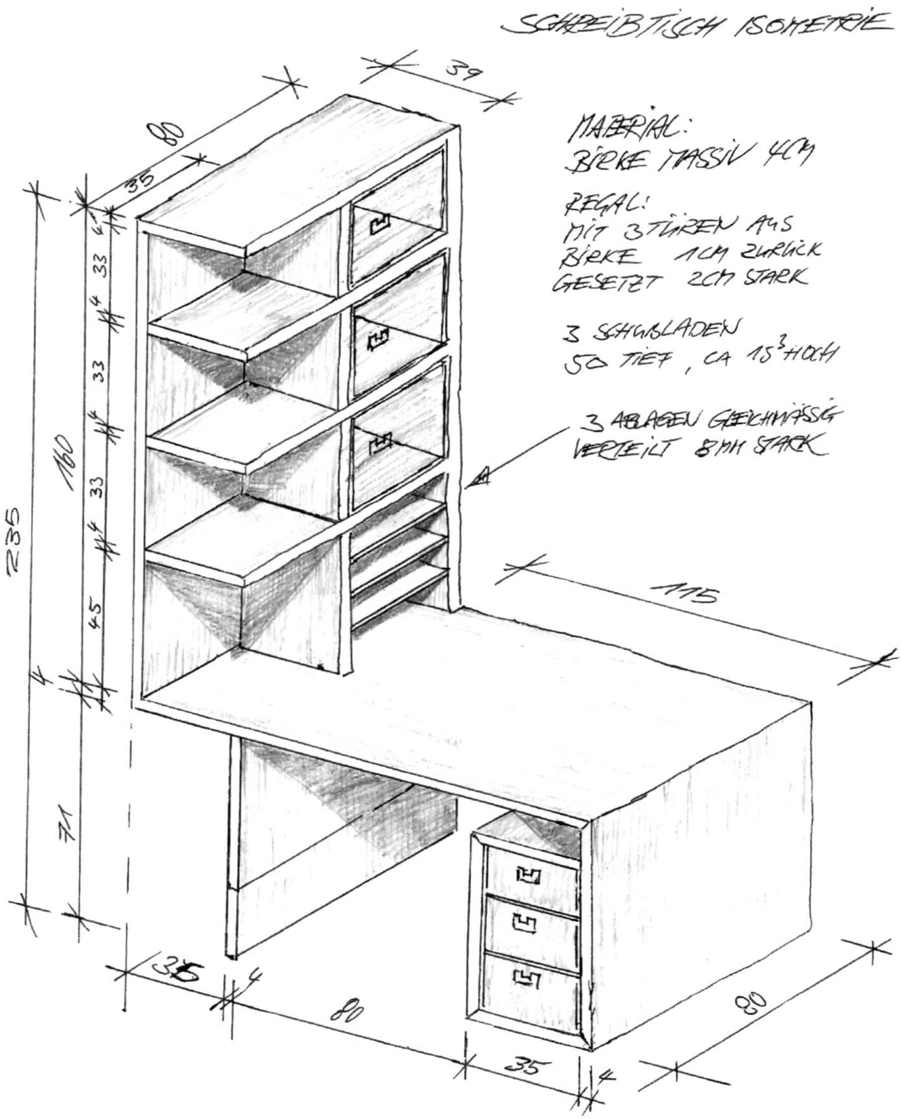
SCHREIBTISCH ISOMETRIE
MATERIAL:
BIRKE MASSIV 4CM
REGAL:
MIT 3 TÜREN AUS
BIRKE 1CM ZURÜCK
GESETZT 2CM STARK
3 SCHUBLADEN
50 TIEF, CA 15 HOCH
3 ABLAGEN GLEICHMÄSSIG
VERTEILT 8MM STARK

70.1.A
Photograph
© Axel Hollmann 2019

70.1
Desk with Shelf
2002

70.2.A
Photograph

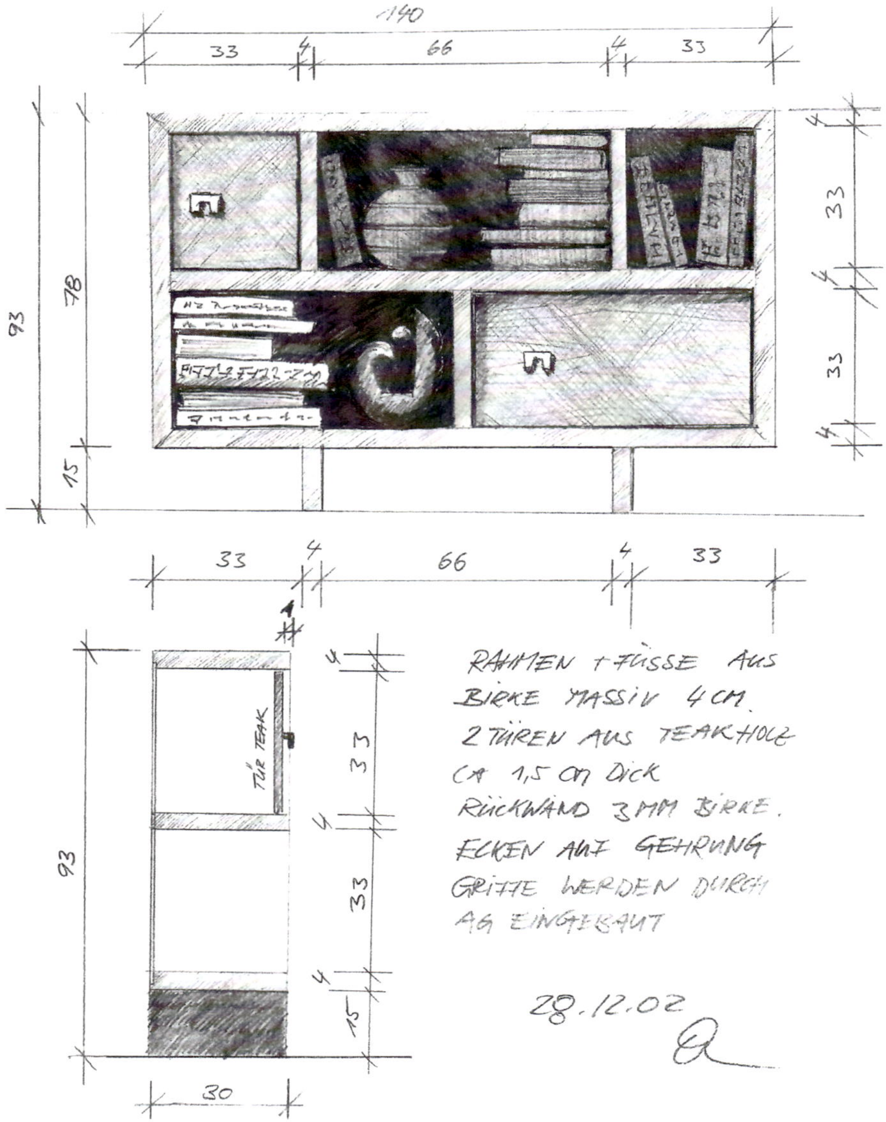

70.2
Sideboard
2002

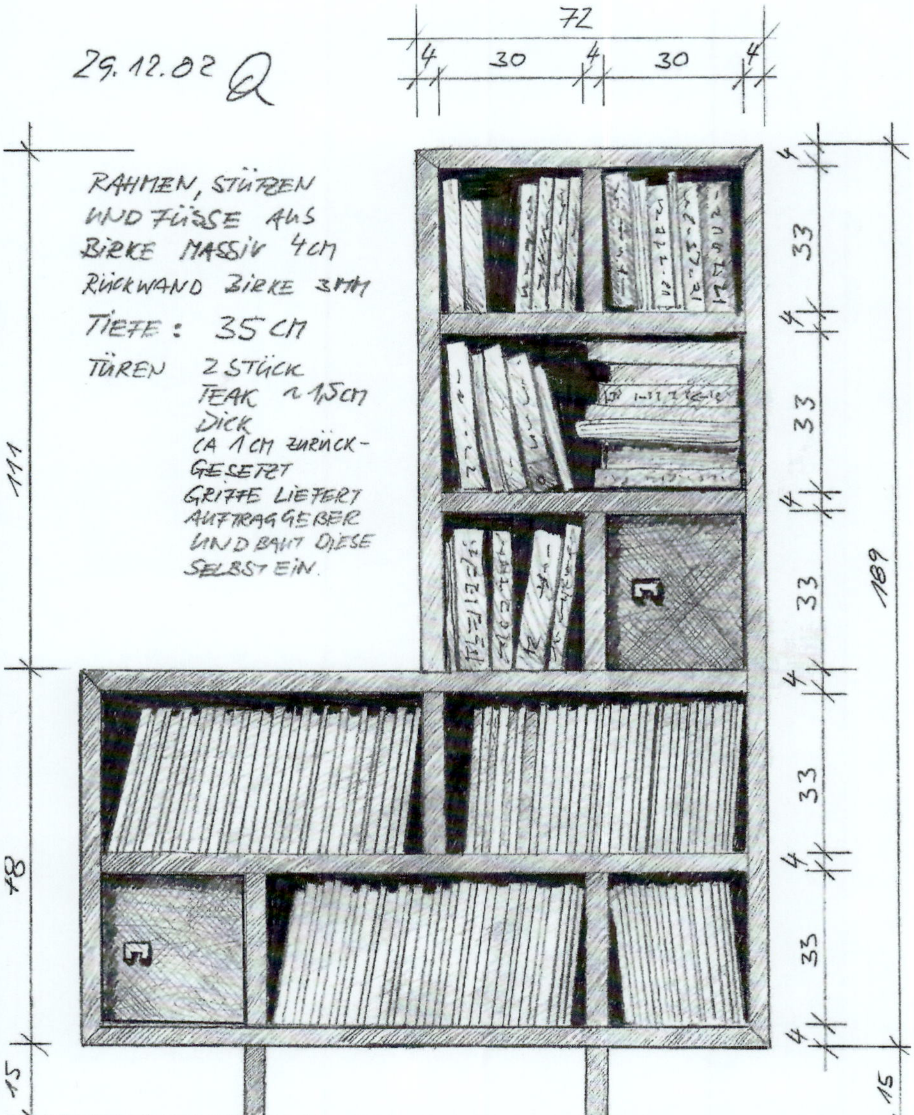

70.3.A
Photograph
© Axel Hollmann 2019

70.3
High Shelf
with Sideboard
2002

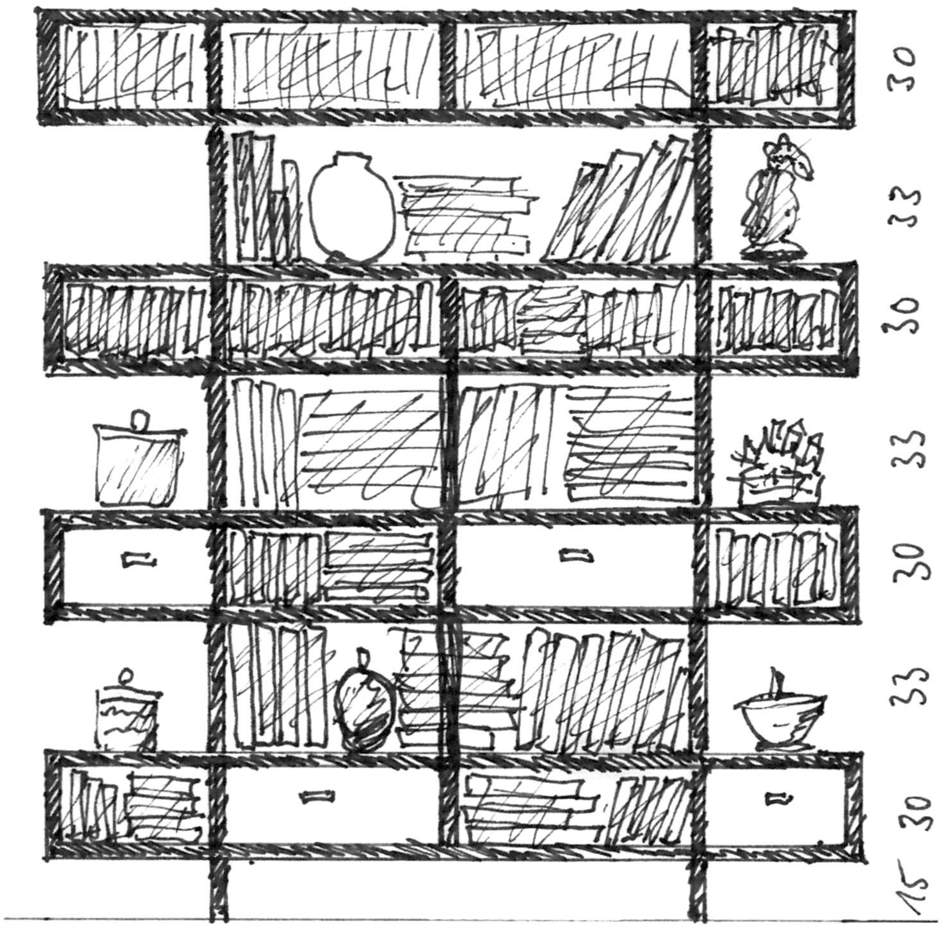

70.4
Open High Shelf
2002

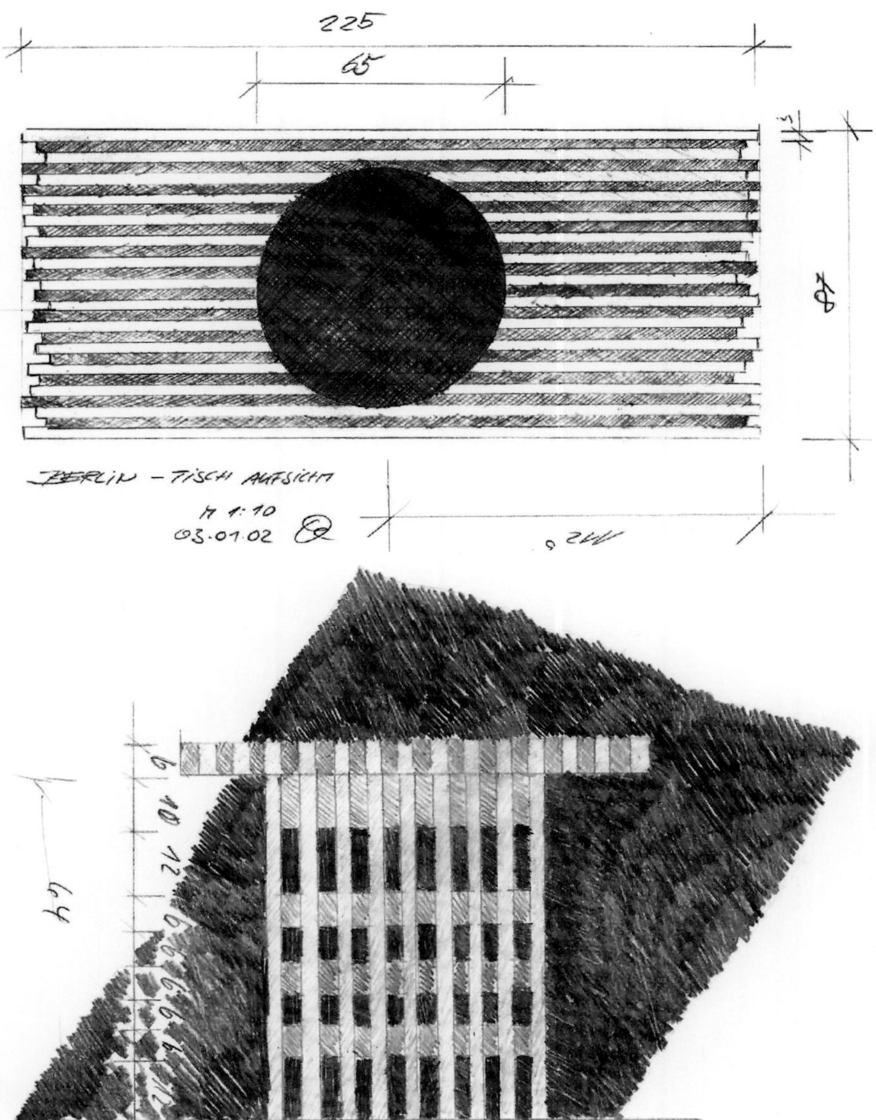

71.1–2
Berlin East-West Table
2002

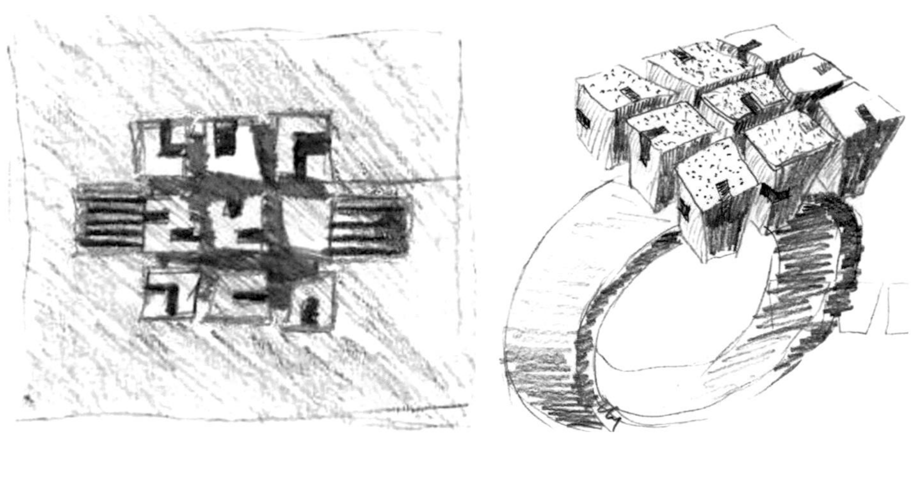

72.1–2
Ring
2004

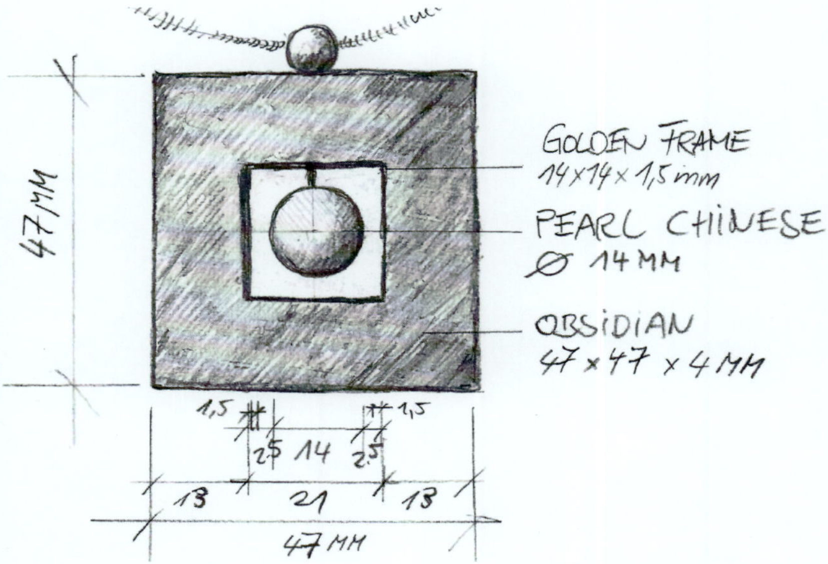

73.1.A
Photograph of the realized pendant (2015)
© Axel Hollmann 2019

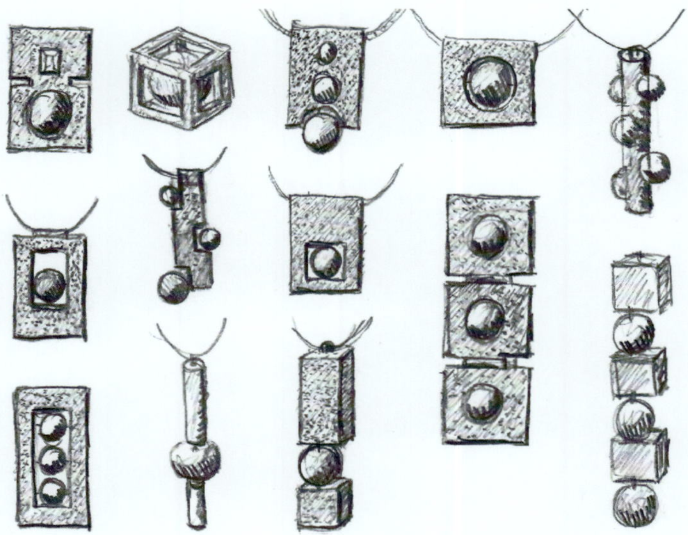

73.1 and Var. 73.2–14
Pendant for a Necklace
2015

CATALOG

SCULPTURES + IDEAS IN STONE Ideas in Stone · Stone Sculptures · Plant Sculptures Stone-Plant Sculptures · Other Sculptures **LANDSCAPE ARCHITECTURE + COMPETITIONS** Competitions · Show Gardens + Exhibitions · Landscape Architecture **MIXED THEMES** Graphic Art · Sculpture · Applied Art

CATALOG PREFACE

The catalog section provides more detailed information on the drawings in the picture section, reproduced in three chapters.

The drawings are numbered consecutively, from catalog number 1 to 73. Drawings presenting several variants on a subject are marked with sub-numbers and 'Var.' (variant abbreviated), e.g. Birdbaths Cat. 3, Var. 1–4.
Projects in which several drawings represent different aspects of a subject are marked with consecutive sub-numbers, e.g. 41.1–9.

Then the number of the page, on which the respective work is found in the picture part, is indicated.
This is followed by the title and the year in which the drawing was made and, if applicable, the location for which a design was created, as well as an indication as to whether or not a realization was carried out. In the third chapter, Mixed Themes, it is stated where the drawings were made.

A brief description then provides detailed, mainly technical information on the drawings. This is followed by explanations by Udo Dagenbach of his intentions regarding the individual designs.

Realized works are depicted photographically in the picture section. Such illustrations are not marked numerically, but alphabetically (e.g. 20.A). A few computer-generated diagrams (renderings) are added to mostly unrealized works, which are therefore easier to visualize. Finally, special features, such as awards, are mentioned.

SCULPTURES + IDEAS IN STONE

Ideas in Stone

1. Var. 1 and 2
Page 24–25

Birdbaths Plant Cell and Mandelbrot Set
1991
For a schoolyard, Berlin, Germany

Realized in 1991, Berlin, Germany

Black-and-white top view drawings (pencil) for each of the two motifs, the plant cell with cross section above it.

This was designed for the second project we planned and realized in the 1990s. I was impressed by the beautiful structure of plant cells and the Mandelbrot set, a phenomenal structure from fractal geometry. The stone sculpture was done in Saxon granite, still found in quarries in the former GDR.

1.A and B
Realized Birdbath Plant Cell,
realized Birdbath Mandelbrot Set
1991

2. Var. 2
Page 26

Italian Fountain
1999
For Prerow, Germany

Not realized

Three black-and-white pencil drawings: a descriptive illustration, a top view with material details, and a sectional drawing of the fountain with technical and material details.

Concept for a stone fountain for a hotel on the Baltic coast.

3. Var. 1–4
Page 27–30

Birdbath Designs
2002

Not realized

Eight colored design drawings (pencil and watercolor) of four square birdbaths with different geometric designs, each with top view, section and diagonal view, as well as dimensions. Version 3 with technical specifications for the stone.

The idea of designing birdbaths came to me, because as a young man I had made some by hand in red sandstone. I found only few appropriate birdbath designs. Most were not usable by the birds—too deep, no landing platform, etc. The birds are the clients, they should be comfortable with our design. And the design should also please us as an element in our garden.

4
Page 31

Birdbath *Labyrinth*
A later version of the previous series
2002

Not realized

Two black-and-white design drawings (pencil): a view with points of the compass, a section with dimensional, material, and surface treatment details, and the name of the stimulus: a model from Compiègne, approx. 17th century.

A special idea for the birdbath series. I like labyrinths, and the small version provided an opportunity to play.

5. Var. 1–8
Page 32–37

Stone Bench Design
Eight variants
2002

Not realized

24 black-and-white pencil drawings: graphic examination of the shape and material of stone benches in descriptive illustrations, with measurements, as well as possible materials (Jura and/or dolomite); in addition, consideration of surface treatment and material change between the two types of stone. Bench No. 3 shows a variant with a wooden seat inlay.

I realized the possibilities of the so-called diamond wire saw, which can do any cut—which is defined by CAD and can be repeated as often as desired. This offered completely new possibilities that I wanted to explore, which is why the series was designed.

6
Page 38–39

Lens Fountain
2003
For Rathenow, Germany

Not realized

Two black-and-white drawings (pencil) of a lenticular fountain on supports, with eight fountain nozzles on the top side. Top and side view.

The fountain design was developed as part of a competition for the city of Rathenow in the former GDR, on the site of an important factory for lenses and other optical instruments. Polished granite was recommended as the material for its execution.

7
Page 40

Land-Shape-1 **black slate**
2004

Not realized

Black-and-white drawing (pencil) of a circular fountain made of black slate: side and top view, with measurements.

The idea was developed for a stone fountain. The natural or broken surface contrasts with the shape, and the water comes out of a golden sphere—quite fifties in mood. It could be done on a larger or smaller scale.

8. Var 1–2
Page 41

Cut Stone Sculpture
2006

Not realized

Three black-and-white idea sketches (pencil): two cuboids, top view, diagonal view; one half-sphere, side view.

In quarries I had seen many left-over rocks shaped by stone processing machines.
I had the idea of using the diamond saw blade for cutting, then leaving some of the stone and filling up the rest with crushed stone and gravel, and planting grasses.

9
Page 42–43

Three-Country Fountain
Euregiobrunnen
2009
For Aachen, Germany

Not realized

Two black-and-white sketches (pencil): a diagram with a view of the monolith and the 45 symmetrically arranged nozzles; and a view showing the border between the three countries as bronze inlay in the stone with the water-spouting nozzles—with dimensional and material data, as well as a description of the basic idea.

As part of a competition for the design of a school in the center of the city of Aachen in Germany, we wanted to design a fountain in the axis of a square.
The idea was to show the specific situation of this very European spot in the triangle of Germany, the Netherlands, and Belgium. The design shows, on top of a stone block, the lines of the borders of the three countries, resulting in the name Drei-Länder-Brunnen, which translates as Three-country Fountain. It was to be realized in local anthracite basalt lava stone, again using the diamond wire cutting technique.

10
Page 44–45

Drinking Fountain in the Shape of a Pomegranate
2014
For the United World College Dilijan, Armenia

Realized in an unsatisfactory form without Dagenbach's involvement.

Black-and-white design drawing (pencil) with detailed measurements and handwritten description on the right-hand side, including material data, as well as information on the slightly inclined positioning of the pomegranate. The pomegranate is the national symbol of Armenia. The irregular shape of the natural fruit is taken up by the round drinking fountain. The surface is covered with classic Armenian ornamentation, and at one point 'broken open', so that the inside of the fruit, the thirst-quenching pomegranate seeds, become visible.

For the United World College in Dilijan, I created the drinking fountain from red tuff. The idea was that the sepals serve as a set of bronze drinking nozzles. The stone should be adorned with typical ornamental elements from traditional Armenian stone carving—a very old tradition: understanding through touching.

11
Page 46–47

Volcanic Benches and Table
2017
For the Bergehalde Ensdorf
("Halde Duhamel"), Saarland, Germany

Not realized

A red and black idea sketch and a colored idea sketch with annotation and representation of several conceivable forms and arrangement of the seating group. Charcoal and red chalk. The colorful and formally striking seating group is intended for a picnic area on the edge of an abandoned pit heap.

A monument referencing the end of coal mining and its history.
We wanted to create a monument—a large tool, a hammer, hammered into the ground, left behind after the mine was abandoned. The red benches were to be symbolic of glowing pieces of coal in the midst of black coal yet to be burned. That is why we chose completely irregular shapes. The material could have been colored concrete.

11.A and B
Rendering, top and diagonal view

SCULPTURES + IDEAS IN STONE

Stone Sculptures

12
Page 48–49

Inverse Wave
2001
For Bansin, Germany

Realized in stone in 2002, Bansin, Germany (in concrete in 2007 and in bronze in 2008)

Black-and-white design sketch (inkballpen) for a sculpture with pedestal, front and side view, with dimensions.

In Bansin, a small town on the North German Baltic coast, we designed the landscape around a seaside hotel. The entrance to the hotel was at the rear, and the building opposite was not very appealing. So I designed the sculpture to attract the attention of visitors leaving the hotel. It was made from Chinese yellow granite, 1.6 meters in diameter. Later, we copied the model in both bronze and concrete.

12.A and B
Photographs of the realized wave in stone (2002) and in bronze (2008)

13
Page 50–51

Endless Column
2002–2004
For Moscow, Russia

Not realized

Two black-and-white descriptive illustrations of the endless column: in a landscape outside the city of Moscow, as well as a black-and-white design drawing with dimensions and technical data for the integration of a light beam high up on the column (in the manner of a lighthouse). Pencil.

In 2002, I started to think about the idea of creating an endless column of stone cylinders of a similar diameter piled up to a height of 15–20 meters.
The basic idea came from the possibilities presented by the diamond wire saw system. It is easy to create a swing cut and copy it to the next stone cylinder.
I thought of every cylinder, each one made from a different type of stone as representing a generation. Each generation has to take on the profile of the previous generation, and then hand on a specific profile to the next one. We cannot escape from that, it is an endless process.

14
Page 52–53

Stone Ball Sculpture
2012

Not realized

Black-and-white idea sketch and colored descriptive illustration.
The Stone Ball Sculpture is characterized by spheres built one on top of the other, becoming smaller and smaller towards the top. The column creates the impression of rising infinitely into the sky, up to the last tiny ball disappearing out of sight. The black-and-white idea sketch (pencil) shows the ball column in a dead, hollow tree stump. In the colored illustration the ball column stands on a pedestal in the shape of a hemisphere.

In one project, a rotten tree trunk was standing in the central axis of a castle in northern Germany. I was looking for a sculpture which could be installed in the rotten trunk, growing out of its center.
The project failed, and so I tried to realize the project on a much larger scale.
The main idea was a construction with wooden play elements like those we used to have as kids.

14.A
Rendering of the Stone Ball Sculpture

SCULPTURES
+ IDEAS IN STONE

Plant Sculptures

15. Var. 1–4, 6–9, 11–13
Page 54–64

Plant Sculptures
2001–2002

Not realized

22 black-and-white sketches (pencil) of ideas and design drawings for eleven different plant sculptures, partly with descriptive illustrations (Object 4, Object 6–7, Object 12–13). Object 9 with sectional drawing, object 13 with top view. The drawings contain measurements as well as details of the recommended plants, such as hornbeam, privet, yew, box, and hawthorn.

In 2001–2002 I thought about developing topi- ary ideas—or let's say plant sculptures —that are more than the classical repertoire that we know. I produced a long series, until I thought things were repeating themselves. The nurseries I showed them to were impressed but none of them started to do it. We are a conservative business and innovations take a long time...

16
Page 65

Plant Sculpture *Quill*
2004

Not realized

Three black-and-white idea sketches (pencil) for a plant sculpture in the form of a quill in a square inkpot: side and top view, descriptive illustration with dimensions and recommended plants.

In 2004, I developed a variation with more dramatic elements, with horns or feathers, which could be arranged in groups.

17
Page 65

Plant Sculpture *Stag Beetle Ball*
2004

Not realized

Black-and-white, inscribed idea sketch (pencil) for a group of plant sculptures, spherical, with a sitting sickle (boxwood ball with outgrowth).

Plant sculpture with ball-shaped base and extreme pair of horn, that can be planted in a group of fighting or dancing figures.

18. Var. 1–6
Page 66–69

Eurobonsai
2005

Not realized

Six black-and-white idea sketches (pencil): Eurobonsai, small trees in different pots. (To illustrate the suggestion, a lithograph from the garden art museum Schloss Fantaisie in Eckersdorf is shown, Friedrich Küchelbecker: The lime tree in Donndorf near Bayreuth. Around 1840.)

Seeing all the Japanese bonsais, I thought it needed a response which was closer to European culture, to the dramatic trees in early Dutch paintings and in the paintings of the German Romantics.
So this series of Romantic Bonsais—or let's say Eurobonsais—was created.

SCULPTURES
+ IDEAS IN STONE

Stone-Plant Sculptures

19
Page 70–71

Surrealistic Stone-Plant Sculpture
2001–2002
For Bad Zwischenahn, Germany

Realized and dismantled 2001–2002
Bruns Nursery, Bad Zwischenahn, Germany

Colored drawing (pencil and watercolor): top view

In 2002, this stone-plant sculpture was realized in front of the administrative building of the North German Bruns Nursery.
It was originally created from Jurassic marble, with a natural 'coastline' and boxwood plants.

19.A and B
Photographs of the realized plant sculpture, diagonal view and detail
2002

20
Page 72

Cone-shaped Stone-Plant Sculpture
2002
For Bad Zwischenahn, Germany

Realized in 2002
Bruns Nursery, Bad Zwischenahn, Germany

Black-and-white pencil sketch: front view of the conical stone and plant sculpture, with dimensions and material details, as well as details of the surface treatment of the stone.

In 2002, the company Franken Schotter from South Germany, which produces Jurassic marble, asked Bruns Nursery in North Germany to do a joint project showing the possibilities of both their products. One of the ideas was this cone-shaped stone-plant sculpture. We used Jurassic marble to create the masonry base, and we added a hornbeam cone on the top.

20.A
Photograph of the realized stone-plant cone.
2002

21
Page 73

Vertical Ellipsoid
2002

Not realized

Colored design drawing: front and top view (pencil and colored pencil).
On the right, a human figure is suggested, to show the proportions.

I had the idea of lifting the stone-plant sculpture into the vertical, as a hybrid column. The stone, a diamond wire-cut limestone, is combined with a yew hedge plant. The total height was to be 2.40 meters.

22
Page 74–75

Cubic Stone-Plant Sculpture
2002
For Bad Zwischenahn, Germany

First realized in 2002, Bruns Nursery
Bad Zwischenahn, Germany.

In the meantime, several copies were realized, e.g. at the United World College in Dilijan, Armenia.

Three-part technical black-and-white drawing (pencil) with top view, view A and B with dimensional data, on the right also data on material, including surface treatment, foundation, and installation.

From the series for the Bruns tree nursery and the Franken Schotter company I developed a minimalistic garden sculpture, intended as a European version of a Zen garden—nothing else to add, nothing to omit. The sculpture—with the dimensions 1.3 x 1.3 x 1.3 meters—is now located on the Prince of Wales Embankment of the United World College in Dilijan, Armenia.
Yew was replaced by Buxus sempervirens (box tree).

22.A–D
Photographs of the realized
Stone-Plant Sculpture
2002

Design Award Winner 2017, silver.
German Design Award Winner 2018, gold.

23
Page 76–77

Ball-shaped Stone-Plant Sculpture
2002
For Bad Zwischenahn, Germany,

Realized in 2002, Bruns Nursery
Bad Zwischenahn, Germany,
and in 2006, Vilnius, Lithuania.

One black-and-white, one colored technical drawing with measurements.
The first illustrates, besides details of the plant-stone ball, the anchoring in the ground by means of a metal rod.
Lead and colored pencil.

In the series for the Bruns Nursery and the Franken Schotter company I developed the same idea as with the cube but for a ball, which was realized in Bad Zwischenahn, Germany (dismantled) and in Vilnius in a private garden.

The ball has a diameter of 1.2 meters.
The stone is Jurassic limestone.

23.A
View of the realized Stone-Plant Sculpture
2002

24
Page 78–79

Ariadne's Thread
2003
For Üselitz, Isle of Rügen, Germany
(outpost of the International Horticultural Exhibition Rostock)

Realized in 2003

Black-and-white design drawing (pencil), top view of the ground sculpture.

In 2003, I was asked by the owners of the ruins of Üselitz Castle on the island of Rügen in the Baltic to contribute a work for the outpost of the international garden show in the city of Rostock. I had the idea of a boxwood labyrinth, but did not have the money for it and could not find sponsors. So I thought up a more special idea.
I designed the fragment of a labyrinth— a part of Ariadne's thread leading into the center. I placed a regular boulder, which I found on the site, in the center and covered it with 24-karat gold leaf. The surrounding area is covered with local flintstone gravel. Every labyrinth has a goal. Here the goal is a gold-covered regular boulder. The question is what you see— the golden coat, or the stone?

24.A–C
Photographs of the realized labyrinth
2003

25
Page 80–81

Halved Erratic Blocks
Interwoven with Willows
2005–2006

Not realized

Three descriptive illustrations, one (2005) colored in gold leaf, the others (2006) in black-and-white, one of them inscribed '3 halbierte Findlinge'.

After the golden boulder in Ueselitz (Cat. 24, Ariadne's Thread), I developed the idea of cut boulders stacked and arranged and bound together by steadily growing willow trees or bushes.

26
Page 82–83

Rectangular Cube
2006
For Vilnius, Lithuania

Realized in 2006, Vilnius, Lithuania

Black-and-white design drawing (pencil), front view of the standing stone-plant sculpture.

In 2006, a private client in Vilnius, Lithuania, asked for a sculpture to block the view between the security booth and the outdoor terrace.
I designed a rectangular stone-plant sculpture, which consists half of Jura marble and half of yew (Taxus media Hicksii).

26.A and B
Photographs of the realized
Rectangular Cube
2006

27
Page 84–85

Flying Stone Discus
2008
For Vilnius, Lithuania

Realized in 2008, Vilnius, Lithuania

Two black-and-white design drawings (pencil), each with main and side view, as well as indications of dimensions and material, stone and bronze content, and surface treatment.

In 2008, I had the idea of creating a flying discus, the upper half made of stone, the lower of yew plants. Two thin steel rods lead from the center of the stone into the ground, hidden by the small young yew plants planted below the stone. A central bronze plate visually connects both elements.
It is still effective after ten years.
The client loves sculpture and wanted something unique.
The installation was done in a private garden in Vilnius, Lithuania.

27.A
Photograph of the realized
Flying Stone Discus
2008

Other Sculptures

28
Page 86–87

Railway Track Sculpture
(Competition 'Poetic Place—2 Track Lines')
2006/2008
For Berlin, Germany

Not realized

Two black-and-white descriptive illustrations (ink pens) with annotations. One showing the steel sculpture from an aerial perspective, the second, the side view, with the eight rails on the one hand as a loop, on the other hand in a wild, free gesture reaching into the sky.

In the last decade many parks have been developed on former railway property. I had the idea of turning a double railway track into a sculpture, having read a book in which a bombed railway track was described: *"The tracks were twisted like noodles and looked as if they were like hands stretched out into the sky."*
So two parallel tracks were cut and connected in a looping style. The redundant tracks twist into the sky. The crushed stones between the tracks form a circle, which is cambered about one meter.
The ideal background would be birches.

29. Var. 1–6
Page 88

Ideas for an Award Trophy
Green Music Award
2007

Not realized

Six black-and-white idea sketches (pencil). Variant 29.5 with front and side view.

One day, my wife, who is in the entertainment management business, told me about an idea to create a global green music award. It was to reward efforts to reduce the ecological footprint in the music business. I immediately began with the idea of mixing wood and glass.

30
Page 89

Steel Nest for Pine Trunks
2009

Not realized

Black-and-white descriptive illustration (pencil) of a light pine forest, with one of the trunks showing the round steel-rod object.

In a dense pine tree forest, I saw a squirrel's nest, and thought it would make an interesting sculpture, if arranged as a stainless steel rod nest.

31.1 and 2
Page 90–91

Two Stone Objects:
Krems Wall Wheel and Krems Wall Onion
2010
For Krems, Austria

Not realized

31.1 Krems Wall Wheel: black-and-white design drawing, front and side view.
31.2 Krems Wall Onion: black-and-white illustration with annotation, dimensions, material structure, and foundation.
Both ink pen.

In 2007, we won the first Daylight Spaces Architecture and Design Award of the Danube University in Krems, Austria (Cat. 41). The award was a four-week artist-in-residence grant at the university. Because it was impossible for me to spend four weeks away from my office, I tried to prepare ideas in case it happened.
Historically, the city of Krems is a very interesting spot. I was fascinated by the onion-shaped church rooftops and the natural quarry stone masonry.
One idea was the 'Krems Wall Wheel', a huge, meter-wide, minimum 1.5-meter high disc, with a viewing hole in the center. The other idea was a sculpture to be placed in the open landscape and shaped like the rooftops of the local churches.
The top was to be made from regular copper rods, 3 meters in diameter, and 2 meters high without the top.

32
Page 92–93

Stage Design for a Sculpture of the Commendatore (Don Giovanni)
2010

Not realized

Two black-and-white drawings (pencil): an idea sketch with several variations and details, as well as an illustration of the sculpture of the Commendatore on a stage.

The design was developed in conversation with a friend of mine, the very successful stage designer Manfred Gruber, who developed a design for Mozart's opera Don Giovanni, in which a sculpture of the Commendatore was to be used.

33.1 and 2
Page 94–95

Palm Tree and Strelitzia Sculptural Mobiles
2014
For the old orangery in Gorki Park
Moscow, Russia

Not realized

Two black-and-white design drawings (ink pen) for an artificial palm tree and an artificial strelitzia with annotation: details of the pedestal or trunk of the kinetic sculptures, dimensions, material, anchoring in the ground, possible planting; at the upper end of the pedestal is the swivel joint, which the steel palm fronds or Strelitzia blossom sit on.

In 2012, we were asked to do the design of a 2.8-hectare park around the old orangery in Gorki Park, Moscow, together with our friends and partners from the natureform company, Moscow.

The park was to be a summer showplace for the yew and boxwood topiary, which in Western Europe we can show throughout the year, but in Moscow need to be stored in a cold glasshouse in winter.
So we thought about sculptural features that could stay outside in winter, rising out of the winter snowscape.
The idea of sculptural mobiles with plant themes came up.
One was the 8.5-meters high sculpture of a palm tree consisting of a mobile steel top and a masonry stem, with flat natural stone and a concrete core.
The stem should be planted with frost-resistant saxifrage or sedum. A botanical sculpture referring to the long tradition of plant collections all over the world.
The second idea for our Gorki Park project was a stainless steel strelitzia on top of a cone-shaped thuja stem.
The mobile could work throughout the winter, and the frost-resistant plant would be an evergreen stem for it.

34. Var. 1 and 2
Page 96–97

Gneissic Rock Houses
2016
For the North Italian/South Alpine region

Not realized

Two versions of black-and-white design drawings on black backgrounds (various ink pens).
34.1 An illustration of two gneissic houses standing one behind the other, with a circular opening, circumferential information on material and connection to local tradition, construction, and dimensions.
34.2 Below, an illustration of two differently shaped gneiss houses (triangular with one-sided curve to the ground as well as irregular trapezoid), above, a side and a top view with indication of scale.

On a long holiday in northern Italy, around Lago di Orta, I was once more fascinated by the nicely done masonry work in the everyday architecture. The old houses and masonry skill are no longer needed, as modern techniques have pushed them into the past. I thought about a sculpture, or monument, which would pay respect to this tradition and art of construction.
The idea was that the construction would have no logical purpose, other than the appreciation of the material and the art of masonry.

35. Var. 1–3
Page 98–99

Amorphous Aluminium Sculptures
2018
For a residence in Moscow, Russia

Var. 35.3 realized in 2019 in the courtyard of the residence

Three black-and-white illustrations (ink pen) with annotation for the originally intended site and material.
35. Var. 3 with designation of the point at which a mirrored version of the sculpture could be placed, thus doubling it.

In 2018, we did a design for the gardens of the so-called A-residence project, a courtyard with high-end apartments in Moscow. The courtyard is on top of the underground parking garage.
So I thought of a sculpture made of aluminium, a material regularly used in Russian Art. It is light and can be flexible. Height around 3.5 meters, consisting of two identical parts.

35.A
Realized 3D print model of the sculpture
2019

LANDSCAPE ARCHITECTURE + COMPETITIONS

Competitions

36. Var. 1–3
Page 102–103

Three Proposals for an Observation Tower
2010
For the Schliersbergalm,
Bavarian Alps, Germany

Not realized

Three black-and-white illustrations (pencil): inscribed illustration of one of the three design variants, the other two as design drawings only.

In 2010, a private hotel owner asked real estate experts to develop his entertainment-focused hotel on the Schliersberg Alm, a winter skiing and summer hiking destination in the Alps. Teams were asked to develop concepts for the location.
One was to erect a very natural lookout tower affording a panoramic view of the city of Munich in the distance.
I thought of using whole trees from the area around the tower and developed three versions using industrial metal stairs.

37.1–6
Page 104–111

Former Cattle Auction Hall Memorial for deported and murdered Thuringian Jews
2018
For Weimar, Thuringia, Germany

Not realized

Second price in the competition

Seven illustrations (various ink pens): two site plans, two sectional illustrations on a black background, one illustration of information board in the woods; the two illustrations with black background showing front and side views of the monolith (with audio-visual information about the place and its history) with figures.

During the Nazi regime, around 800 Thuringian Jews were deported and murdered—only one survived.
Consequently, the city of Weimar decided to organize a competition to remember this event. The Jews were rounded up, and deported by train from a former cattle auction hall, which was burned down by young men in 2015 around the time of Adolf Hitler's birthday.
We participated in the competition with the media artist Boris Hars-Tschachotin and the exhibition design office Molitor.
We decided to create a concrete railway wagon out of which the names of the murdered Jews are whispered. Inside you would see the fire of the burning hall, symbolic of the final fate of the victims.
I was really disappointed to receive second prize. The argument was that the design was too 'strong' for the citizens, and that focusing on the fire of the burning hall was either too 'hard' or wrong.
But that was exactly what we wanted to do. I think the decision was misguided. The victims need respect, and the living have to

deal with it—a 'light' version of a memorial is an attitude I do not understand.
I did the whole competition in a newly developed black-and-white sketching mode, which helps me to concentrate on the main issue without working on the background. A kind of inverse etching.

37.A
Site plan, mixed media

LANDSCAPE ARCHITECTURE + COMPETITIONS

Show Gardens + Exhibitions

38
Page 112–113

Fabergé Egg Garden
2013
For Mikhailovsky Garden, St. Petersburg, Russia (Plantomania Flower Exhibition, Contest at the Imperial Gardens of Russia Festival 2013)

Realized in 2013

Black-and-white drawing (ink pen), top view of the oval ground plan, with depiction of the plant and soil design elements that give this charming show garden the appearance of a Fabergé egg.

In 2013, the Bruns Nursery asked us to take part in the Plantomania garden show in the Mikhailovsky Garden at the Russian Museum in St. Petersburg. The themes were created around the 400th anniversary of the Romanov family. Our theme was 'Beauty will save the world'. As I knew about the Russian people's love for the famous Fabergé eggs, I created a garden with gold applied to the hedges and topiary, as if it might be wallpaper in a room. The work was there for just one week, and won the prize for the best show garden in its category. I will never forget the white nights during this event.

38.A
Interior view of the realized garden
2013

38.B and C
Renderings, top view and detail

First prize Plantomania Flower Exhibition Contest, St. Petersburg, 2013

39.1–2
Page 114–115

Arc for Lovers
2014
For Gorki Park, Moscow, Russia
(Moscow Festival of Gardens and Flowers)

Realized in 2014

Two black-and-white illustrations (pencil): a two-part, inscribed drawing with top view and view of the arbor on a parabola-shaped ground plan and its surroundings, indications of dimensions and plants; an inscribed top view, schematic of the steel arch with depiction of the ground vegetation and surroundings.

In 2014, on the occasion of a fair in Moscow, I talked with our friend Elena Dubnova about taking part in the Moscow flower show in Gorky Park. The spot we could use was not big, so we thought about maximizing its use in terms of effect. We experimented with strong perspective views. Finally, we thought of having a bench for two persons, and we called it *Arc for lovers.*

39.A
Interior view of the realized arc
2014

Award as best show garden for small city gardens.

40
Page 116–117

Exhibition Booth Design
2018
For GaLaBau Nuremberg, Germany

Realized in 2018 for Franken Schotter (a natural stone company) at the GaLaBau (fair for urban green and open spaces) Nuremberg, Germany

Black-and-white inscribed drawing of the whole exhibition stand, rich in details, showing a wide range of different stone products and surfaces, also different styles, such as rustic, elegant, playful, as well as different stone furniture; and Cat. 22 (Cubic Stone-Plant Sculpture). Ink pen.

In 2018, the natural stone company, Franken Schotter, asked us to help with the design of their exhibition booth at the landscape gardening fair GaLaBau in Nuremberg, Germany. We had won a German design award in 2018 for a stone-plant sculpture, which had been created with limestone from Franken Schotter. So we installed a smaller version of this sculpture, and integrated ideas on stones for sitting, that could be a replacement for anti-terror barricades in cities.

40.A
Realized booth design

LANDSCAPE ARCHITECTURE + COMPETITIONS

Landscape Architecture

41.1–9
Page 118–125

History Park Former Prison Moabit
Since 1993
Berlin-Moabit, Germany

Realized, completed in 2006

Nine black-and-white drawings:
41.1 Overall plan of the complex.
41.2–4 Several sketches of the central architectural element, the wall passage, and the design of the lock of the park gate.
41.5 Two-part sketch of ideas for an area with shaped trees.
41.6 and 7 Annotated illustrations: courtyard for walks and lowered lawn.
41.8 Annotated illustration: walls.
41.9 Two-part illustration: wall passage, outside and inside view.
Various pens.

In 1849, the Moabit Prison—an almost exact copy of a prison in London—near Berlin's Central Station, was completed. It was destroyed in 1959.
In 1991 we were asked to assess whether the remaining relics should be listed. We were successful and developed and completed the design for a 'History Park' in 1994, 1996, and 2001. My Russian friend Alexander Khomiakov helped me with some excellent ink drawings. The drawings shown here are the ones I made for him as information. The project was very complex, and it was completed in 2006.
When designing the History Park, landscape architecture faced the difficult task of reconciling the burden of the history of an old prison with the need to create a recreational space for the residents: a park as a combination of public space and memorial site. Prisoners' stories told in an architectural garden, with elements of land art and minimal art. Innovative abstract design rather than awkward direct translation.

41.A and B
Photographs of the central architectural element, close-up and overall view
2006

41.C–E
Photograph of the lowered lawn, detail, as well as outside and inside view of the wall passage
2006

German Landscape Architecture Prize BDLA: 1st prize
2007

Daylight Spaces Architecture and Design Competition of the Danube University in Krems, Austria: 1st prize
2007

A-Design Award, Como, Italy—Gold Award
2017

42
Page 126–127

Land Art Design for a Former Runway
1997
For the former runway of the Royal Air Force Station Gatow, Berlin, Germany

Not realized

Large black-and-white drawing (ballpoint pen): one sheet, showing top and bottom views of the landscape design.

The site, in the western part of former West Berlin, was an airport used during the Nazi period and later by the British until the re-

unification of Berlin. In 1997, an urban housing project was planned for the former airfield.
My idea was to create a land art sculpture out of the former runways. At least one of them was to be filled up to form a ramp in the sky by recycling the old runway concrete. A row of Italian poplar trees would describe a line like a frozen movement rising up into the sky.

43
Page 128–129

Mathematical Private Garden
2002
Berlin, Germany

Realized in 2002

Black-and-white design drawing for the small front garden (pencil).

Experimental, small front garden for a family in Berlin, whose daughter is a very talented sculptor. I tried to design the steeply sloping site as a mathematical garden, with a precisely defined place for a sculpture.
I think mathematics is a great tool for organizing life and work, but not art—landscape design is, in the end, far from being a formula for guaranteeing success.

43.A and B
Rendering: site plan, design variant.
Photograph: part of the garden with a sculpture by Elgin Willigerodt.

44.1–6
Page 130–135

Garten von Ehren
2006
For the Garden Center Lorenz von Ehren in Hamburg, Germany

Realized in 2006

Six black-and-white drawings (pencil):
44.1 General plan of the entrance area in front of the new garden center.
44.2 Sectional drawing of the area at the rear of the center, with different designs and a water basin.
44.3 Technical design drawing of the front water basin, with dimensional and material specifications.
44.4 and 5 Two technical drawings of quadrant segments, with cubic and circular plant-gravel sections.
44.6 Design drawing with dimensional data for the rear water basin.

The owner and CEO of the nursery Lorenz von Ehren, established in 1865 in Hamburg, Germany, invited us to enter the competition to design their new high-end garden center, close to their new nursery in Hamburg-Mahlfeld.
We won the competition and were able to create a landscaper's paradise in a really lush space, with many very impressive large and old plants.
At the entrance, I designed an inverse parterre—the plants becoming the decorative gravel element and the gravel representing the plants. To the left, the garden develops in a strictly formal, minimalistic style, and to the right in more playful, organic shapes.
The great Japanese landscape architect Shiro Nakane developed a traditional Japanese pond garden—it was a joy to work together with this master of Japanese gardens.

44.A Aerial photograph of the baroque garden © Arndt Haug
44.B Photograph: detail of the fountain bowl in the front water basin
44.C and D Photographs of the quadrant segments

All photographs 2006

45
Page 136–137

Garden Art Installation *G'Mies Bed*
2008
For the Mies van der Rohe Haus, Berlin, Germany

Realized 2008

Black-and-white design drawing (pencil) with lettering, top view of the four differently designed beds.

The architect Ludwig Mies van der Rohe designed a country house for the art publisher Karl Lemke and his wife Martha, in Berlin-Hohenschönhausen, before emigrating to the United States. In 2000, our office redesigned the garden. In 2006, the house, today an art exhibition space, started doing garden art projects in the Lemkes' former vegetable garden. The first, the G'Mies Bed, was an ironic interpretation of vegetable gardens: a game with herbs and colorful gravel, for example a constructivist herb bed. The work's ambiguous title, G'Mies Bed, is a play on words, referring both to the vegetable and the famous architect's name.
In 2013, we created another installation in the Lemke vegetable garden to mark the 125th birthday of Mies van der Rohe, referencing his destroyed monument to Rosa Luxemburg and Karl Liebknecht.

45.A
Photograph, top view
2008

46.1 and 2
Page 138–139

Private Garden
2008
For a bunker on the Elbe River, Brunsbüttel, Germany

Not realized

Two black-and-white drawings (pencil and ink pen): site plan and illustration of a garden section with hedge blocks at different heights, with sculpture.
The site plan shows a tightly structured garden with a strong geometric emphasis.

At the confluence of the North Sea-Baltic Sea Canal and the Elbe there was an old bunker. A large residential building was erected on the bunker. The surrounding garden was more of a walk through space. It could be seen from close up from a dike open to the public.

47.1 and 2
Page 140–141

Oval Briquette Wall
2009
For the Moabit City Garden, Berlin, Germany

Realized in 2011
(see also Play Equipment Cat. 48.1–4)

Two black-and-white pencil drawings: an illustration in which the structuring 'stones', in the form of egg-shaped charcoal briquettes, are shown in detail, as well as a sketch depicting three linked briquette wall compartments.

Design for a concave wall for the so-called Moabit City Garden, a one–hectare park in Berlin on the site of a former railway freight station (see also Cat. 48.1–4). The concave wall reflects the noise of a nearby road. The 'eggs' are a reference to the egg-shaped coal which was stored there in the old days. It is cast in concrete.

47.A and B
Photographs: detail and outside view of the wall
2011

48.1–4
Page 142–145

Seesaw, Swing, and Hammock: Play Equipment made of Railway Tracks
2009
For the Moabit City Garden, Berlin, Germany

Realized in 2012
(see also Oval Briquette Wall Cat. 47.1 and 2)

Four black-and-white pencil drawings, all inscribed.
48.1 Cruciform twin-seesaw made of railway tracks: view and top view
48.2 Partner Swing: front and side view
48.3 Hammock: front and side.
48.4 Annotated illustration with swing and seesaw, to the right the hammock.

The old freight station in Moabit, Berlin, was for a long time an important part of the infrastructure of this former industrial area. Today, people from more than 60 nations live in the district. The local government decided to create a park around the abandoned freight station. In 2010, we won a competition to design the park. One idea was to use the steel railway tracks as design elements for playground equipment. We bent them into circles and installed swings and hammocks.

48.A and B
Photographs of the partner swing and the hammock.
2012

Dagenbach won first place in the design competition for a park on the former Moabit freight station and realized the Moabit city garden, with the participation of children, youth, and other members of the public.
City Brand and Landscape Award, Milan, Italy, 2017, special mention.

49.1 and 2
Page 146–147

Barbecue Area in Alpine style and Pergola Garden
2009
Samara, Russia

Not realized

Black-and-white site plan and illustration of the country house, with the outdoor dining area under a pergola on the left, and round grill tray on the far left.
Pencil.

A client and enthusiastic hunter in Russia wanted a barbecue area in alpine style. It also had to be usable during the long Russian winter.

50
Page 148–149

Country House Garden
2012
North Caucasus, Georgia

Not realized

Black-and-white site plan of the garden designed around the already existing country house. Ink pen.

Along the old military road from Georgia to Chechnya in Russia, a customer had a country estate that required an extension and conversion with a slightly more 'garden style'. Until then, cows had been happily strolling through the estate, eating everything they could get their teeth into. The property is located around 2,600 meters above sea level. We were asked to design a new country-house-style garden, with an extension to the house including a barbecue area. Apparently, the plan was never realized.

51
Page 150

Private Garden for a Bauhaus-style House
2015
Berlin, Germany

Realized 2015

Black-and-white site plan sketch of the garden, realized on a narrow rectangular plot; front garden with shaped, cut bushes; the main area, behind the house, with large, framed lawn. Ink pen.

The modern Bauhaus-style house of Haas Architects needed a complementary surrounding landscape. The steep garden had many steps, with hedge blocks in different heights structuring the space.

51.A
Photograph: front garden
2015

52
Page 151

Redesign of Elmtree Cottage Garden
2016
Wiltshire, United Kingdom

Not realized

Two versions: one black-and-white (pencil), one colored (colored pencils) site plan, with annotations. Proposal for the redesign of the garden around the Elmtree Cottage (with garage).

In 2016, Tim Flynn, an architect and friend from London, asked me to do a conceptual design for his 16th-century cottage outside London. The challenge was to integrate the designed garden parts with the view from inside the cottage.

53
Page 152–153

Center of a Botanical Garden
2016
Astana, Kazhakstan

Not realized

Black-and-white ink pen drawing, representation of the star-shaped center of the Botanical Garden, in which eight walkways intersect.

In 2016, a friend told me about the newly built Botanical Garden in Astana, Kazakhstan.
We thought of a topiary garden, an exotic garden, and a lookout tower in the middle, where the eight walkways intersect.

53.A and B
Renderings: 53.B showing the central steel-glass structure, that continues the star-shaped intersection into the vertical.

54
Page 154

Private Garden
2018
Templin, Brandenburg, Germany

Completion in process

Black-and-white site plan sketch: garden with the main motif of a curved walkway from the house to the lower end of the property, with handwritten and printed annotations, as well as the legend on the right-hand side. Pencil.

A friend of mine, an architect from Berlin, asked me to join his project for a country house for a family in the picturesque landscape north of Berlin on a lake in the woods. The plot is very steep, with a 5-8 meters drop down to the lake. I decided to create a natural garden with a flower meadow flowing down to the water.
The garden is meant to reinforce the view from the house to the lake.

MIXED THEMES

Graphic Art

55.1 and 2
Page 158–159

Biomorph I and II
1974, Stuttgart, Germany

Two pencil drawings.
55.1 A standing structure consisting of plant and seemingly inorganic parts.
55.2 The larger of the two sheets shows a fantasy plant extending diagonally across the paper.

I had the opportunity of visiting Paris at the age of 17 with my school class. The Centre Pompidou had just been opened, and I was so delighted by the French surrealists—the work of Marcel Duchamp especially impressed me a lot. The drawings followed soon after.

56.1 and 2
Page 160–163

Garden Views, Japan:
56.1 Part of the Garden at the Shoden-ji Temple, Kyoto
56.2 Part of the Garden at the Entsu-ji Temple, Kyoto
1982, Tokyo, Japan

Two black-and-white pencil drawings, with views from the temples, showing impressions of the famous Japanese garden art.

The works were created during my study visit to Japan in 1982–1983.

The Shoden-ji Garden, a dry landscape garden in Kyoto, Japan, had been such an inspiring place for me that I needed to do a drawing. Instead of gravel they used sand—the older tradition. The Entsu-ji Garden impressed me a lot, as it is an example of the so-called borrowed landscape style shakei—Mount Hiei in the background is part of the garden—a very strong idea.

57
Page 164

Haniwa and Isolator
1983, Tokyo, Japan

The artistic black-and-white pencil drawing combines an old porcelain isolator with two Haniwa figures—Japanese clay statues—as the main motif. The group of three stands on threateningly crumbling ground in the foreground, which may have been caused by an earthquake. In the background is a Shōji wall, typical of Japanese houses.

During my internship in Japan in 1982– 1983, I found a ceramic isolator on a construction site. I was impressed by its shape, which looked like an archaic phallic sculpture.
I saw the so-called Haniwa clay figures in a museum and placed them together with the isolator in an earthquake landscape.

58
Page 165

Portrait of a Zen Buddhist Priest
1983, Tokyo, Japan

Impressive black-and-white pencil drawing: head-and-shoulders portrait, characterized by striking lines and large, graded shaded areas.
I drew this portrait of a Zen Buddhist priest from a Japanese sketch. I forgot what period he lived in. His face tells his story, without need of a book or a film.

59.1 and 2
Page 166–167

Scissors' Ballet
1984, Berlin, Germany

Black-and-white sketch of an idea, movement study (ink print), and a black-and-white linocut, in which Japanese scissors are reinterpreted as three dynamic dancing figures moving freely on a kind of stage.

In Japan I bought some old-style scissors, which had been crafted at Ueno Park in Tokyo. Their shape inspired me to draw a ballet scene with headless dancers.

60.1 and 2
Page 168–169

Grandma Maria and Grandpa August
1985 and 1986, Stuttgart, Germany

A linocut plate and a linocut: portraits of Dagenbach's maternal grandparents.

My grandmother Maria and grandfather August were both born in southern Germany. I lived with them for five years. It was only at the age of 24 that I understood that their life—which included getting through two world wars—had very much marked their faces. I am glad that they had happy days in their old age. Later, I called my grandparents' generation 'the silent old men and women'.

61.1 and 2
Page 170–171

Rocks in Norway:
61.1 Coastline in southern Norway close to Larvik
61.2 Labradorite quarry in southern Norway
1986, Larvik, Norway

Observational drawings—one colored, and one in black-and-white pencil and charcoal —both depicting, in bold strokes, large rock areas in the wild in Norway: granite on the coast, labradorite in a quarry.

The southern Norwegian coastline of Ula Strand (Ula beach), close to Larvik, made a strong impression on me: a heavily eroded landscape, formed by the forces of ice age glacial erosion.

In 1986, we worked on the fountain sculpture at the Botanical Museum in Berlin. At that time long drilling traces determined the look of the quarry—today it is only diamond wire saws, leaving traces that are flat like cubist structures. So this drawing documents an historic phase.

62.1–3
Page 172–174

Sketches for Kids:
Fish and Balloon,
Fish, Elephant Couple
1992, Berlin, Germany

The fish pictures are cheerful, colorful watercolor paintings; the work with the pink elephant pair (highlighter) is characterized by strong contrast and contouring with black ink pen.

It took quite a time to make these drawings look as if they were done by chance.

63.1–3
Page 175

Turtle Sketch and Snail Shell Sketches
(Mathilde is the name of the pet in the German Embassy in N'Djamena, Chad)
2016, N'Djamena, Chad, Africa

Two illustrations, white on black background: snail shells, front and rear view. Drawing of the top of a turtle, white on black background. Inkball pen.

In 2016, we visited N´Djamena, the capital of Chad in Africa. We went there with SDARC architects from Berlin to gather information on our project for the German Embassy of the Republic of Chad.
Inside the embassy garden, there was a lone turtle—around 60 years old—called Mathilde, a turtle with a strong character. The whole compound was also full of snail shells, the same type from which I did my first sculpture when I was 18 years old. So Mathilde was the right inspiration for an 'African tableau'.

64.1–6
Page 176

Yucca Sketches
2017, Berlin, Germany

Six illustrations, white on black background, for Dagenbach's essay *Yucca Filamentosa – Die Palmlilie*.
64.1 shows the whole plant with panicle.
64.2–5 details, such as the plant with its root, the fine hairs of the leaves, or a single flower of the panicle. Inkball pen.

For the book *Die Kunst in der Natur* (Art in Nature), which was published by the Mies van der Rohe Haus in Berlin, featuring various artists, art scholars, lecturers, authors, scientists etc., the participants had the opportunity of describing the plants and vegetative structures in the garden around the Mies van der Rohe Haus. For a whole year, the lectures on the selected themes were presented in the gallery, or in the garden, then summarized in the book.
My choice was to write and reflect on the Yucca filimentosa. The drawings were done to illustrate my text.

Also shown in:
Die Kunst in der Natur (Art in Nature)
Series Mies van der Rohe Haus 2, Berlin, 2017, p. 154.

65.1–3
Page 177

Juniper Sketches
2017, Berlin, Germany

Three illustrations, white on a black background, for Dagenbach's essay *Der Wacholder: "Vor dem Wacholder zieht man den Hut"*. (Juniper: Take off your hat to the juniper.)
65.1 shows the scene illustrating the title, plus the annotation; because of the numerous positive qualities, respect and reverence are shown for this plant.
65.2 and 3 show details, such as juniper berries. Ballpoint pen.

Same project as the previous one, but here the plant was juniper. During my research, I was impressed by the story that the Romans used to burn juniper bushes for mystic reasons.

Also appears in:
Die Kunst in der Natur (Art in Nature)
Series Mies van der Rohe Haus 2, Berlin, 2017, p. 226.

MIXED THEMES

Sculpture

66
Page 178–179

'Square Head' Standing on its Feet, on its Head, and Kneeling
1983, Stuttgart, Germany

Realized in 1985 (sandstone)

Sculpture dimensions:
height 44 cm, width 20 cm

Black-and-white movement study (pencil) for the stone sculpture; design drawing for the 'Square Head': a cube with a circular central opening, on it the figure of a human body with arms and legs.
The cube represents the head.

The idea was to create a much bigger sculpture, but I could not get a larger stone, so I did it in sandstone, which was available. Originally, I intended to plant a tree in the head of the sculpture, but due to its small size I scrapped this idea. When the sculpture was finished, I found that it could be positioned in three different ways, without falling over. Not planned, but gratefully accepted...
The shape was influenced by the sculptures around the roofs of the Gothic cathedrals in Freiburg and Strasbourg.

66.A–C
Three photographs of the sculpture, in two different possible positions.

67
Page 180–181

Torso
1984, Stuttgart, Germany

Realized in 1984 in sandstone after a clay model

Sculpture dimensions:
height 67 cm, width 40 cm

Three-part black-and-white sketch (pencil) of the torso, front and side view, as well as a smaller variant on the bottom right.

For this project I took out a sandstone step from a glasshouse in the forestry institute, where my family lived, and replaced it with concrete. I was very strongly influenced by Jean Arp, the Swiss sculptor. I tried to create a torso in which the scale switches, so that you see a completely abstract figure from one side and the torso from the other. That was the time when I first met my wife—an influence I cannot deny.

67.A–C
Photographs of the sculpture, front and side views.
1984

68
Page 182–183

Golden Mask
1985, Stuttgart, Germany

Realized in 1985, carved in sandstone. Gold-plated in 2018

Sculpture dimensions:
height 19 cm, width 33 cm
Design drawing of the mask (ink pen), white on black background, only half the 'face' is executed with a closed eye and strongly stylized eyebrow and forehead. The circular open mouth and nose also included on the right half of the face of the heart-shaped mask. The drawing and its execution are strongly reminiscent of Art Deco.

When I was young I had no money to buy stone, so I had to use what I found along roads and on waste dumps. This project had to be done using a small stone. I was inspired by the sculpture of Constantin Brâncuși and the German sculptor Emy Roeder—my kind of sleeping muse.

68.A–B
Photographs: front view and detail, 2018.

69
Page 184–185

Two-piece Stone Sculpture *Embedded*
2018, Berlin, Germany

Realized in 2018. Two-piece sculpture of gilded sandstone, with sheet steel base

Sculpture dimensions:
height 10 cm, width 17 cm

Top view of the two parts of the sculpture on a square base, with technical description (pencil).

The sculpture was the result of an accident. The original sculpture, made in 1985 of beige sandstone, I made from part of a small wall in a forest, big enough to create a pedestal and the sculpture.
I never really liked the result and banished it to a corner of the balcony. In 2015, it fell down and broke into three pieces. This gave me the chance to make something better out of it. I took two pieces, reshaped them, and then asked a blacksmith to build a new pedestal. A very experienced craftswoman put gold leaf on the two stone pieces, and now it is a flexible sculpture, that can be arranged in different ways, as it is not attached directly to the pedestal.

69.A and B
Photographs of the two-piece, gold-plated sculpture on its new pedestal, 2018.

MIXED THEMES

Applied Art

70.1
Page 186–187

Desk with Shelf
2002, Berlin, Germany

Realized in 2002 in massive 40 mm thick birchwood

Two black-and-white design drawings (pencil) for a desk with shelving on the left side; diagonal view of the furniture, the larger one with dimensions and material specifications (birchwood).

Growing up in a forested environment, the color and smell of wood fascinated me.
I always felt bad living among so many composite materials and missed the heavy wood in our home. When my wife had the idea of moving most of our books on the shelves in the bedroom, this was the kickoff for a set of new furniture which we realized over the following three years.
I decided to use heavy birchwood, because of its density, bright color and availability in the forests around Berlin. The next decision was to use only 40 mm thick wood for all the framework. The thickness guaranteed that it would never bend, like all the cheap, ready-made shelves from our student days.

70.1.A
Photograph
© Axel Hollmann 2019

70.2
Page 188

Sideboard
2002, Berlin, Germany

Realized in 2002 in massive 40 mm thick birchwood

Black-and-white two-part design drawing (pencil) for a low shelf on supports, front and side view, with dimensions and material.

70.2.A
Photograph
© Axel Hollmann 2019

70.3
Page 189

High Shelf with Sideboard
2002, Berlin, Germany

Realized in 2002 in massive 40 mm thick birchwood

Black-and-white design drawing (pencil), front view, with dimensions and material specifica-tions (birch and teak), on one side low, on the other side high shelves.

70.3.A
Photograph
© Axel Hollmann 2019

70.4
Page 190

Open High Shelf
2002, Berlin, Germany

Not realized

Black-and-white design drawing (pencil) for an open shelf unit without side walls; compartments in the lower area with doors; dimensions on the right-hand side.

71.1 and 2
Page 191

Berlin East-West Table
2002, Berlin, Germany

Not realized

Two black-and-white design drawings (pencil) for a table: top and side view, slatted wooden top (alternately light and dark) with central circular inlay; table side supports; strip gratings.

As our living room is orientated in east-west direction, I had the idea to make the table, at which we celebrate dinners with our friends and guests, particularly special. Thus, the form of an endless table with a circle at its center was born, and named after Berlin, where we live.

71.1 - 2
Page 192

Ring
2004, Berlin, Germany

Not realized

Two black-and-white idea sketches (pencil) for a finger ring with a raised square ring plate, on which nine different cubic elements sit.
Top and diagonal view.

During landscape design test sketches, I thought it would be interesting to use this minimalistic design in jewelry.

73.1 and 73. Var. 2 - 14
Page 193

Pendant for a Necklace
2015, Berlin, Germany

73.1 realized in 2015

13 black-and-white idea sketches (pencil) for mostly cubic necklace pendants with one or more pearls. 73.1 black-and-white design drawing with measurements and materials: obsidian with golden frame inside and outside, framing the centrally hanging Chinese pearl.

In 2012, I had the opportunity of presenting our office at an exhibition in Hangzhou, China. On this occasion I bought a nice big pearl for my wife. It was lying around for a time, and then I tried to develop some jewelry with it.
I did a series of test drawings and ended up thinking about using obsidian. Our Armenian project for the United World College Dilijan often led me to visiting a zeolite and obsidian quarry. The black volcanic glass fascinated me greatly. So, the idea for a pearl pendant in an obsidian frame became a reality: Armen, a talented jewelry-maker, realized it very professionally.

73.1.A
Photograph of the realized pendant (2015)

VITA

Name	Udo Hubert Dagenbach
Date of birth	12.08.1958
Place of birth	Stuttgart-Zuffenhausen, Germany
Nationality	German
Family status	Married
Professional qualifications	Dip. Eng., Landscape Design, Technische Universität Berlin Landscape Gardener
Memberships	bdla—Federation of German Landscape Architects IFLA—International Federation of Landscape Architects Federal Foundation for Baukultur (Bundesstiftung Baukultur)
Office address	glaßer und dagenbach garden and landscape architects Breitenbachplatz 17 10781 Berlin, Germany
Office telephone	+49(0)30 61 81 080
Mobile telephone	+49(0)172 92 77 565
Email	info@glada-berlin.de
Website	www.glada-berlin.de

Professional Career

1977–1979	Training as landscape gardener in Stuttgart
1979–1980	Landscaping company in Stuttgart One-man business
1980–1986	Study of landscape design at the Technische Universität Berlin Dip.Eng. Landscape Architecture
1982–1983	Internship and educational travel in Japan Takeshi "Ken" Nakajima—landscape architect, Tokyo Research on and restoration of historical gardens
1983–1985	Guest student at the University of the Arts, Berlin, with the Japanese sculptor Professor Makoto Fujiwara
1984–1987	Working in partnership with the Japanese sculptor Makoto Fujiwara 1985—First prize in the competition for the Federal Institute for Geosciences, Hannover Realized in 1985–1986 (fountain and landscape sculpture) 1986—First prize in the competition for the Botanical Museum, Berlin (fountain)
1985–1988	Freelance work with Manfred Bogisch, Landscape Architecture Firm, Berlin
since 1988	Founding of GBR glaßer und dagenbach with Silvia Glaßer Member of the Berlin Chamber of Architects since 1990 Planning and realization of open-space projects, such as hotels, resorts, parks, business parks, private gardens, school grounds; consultant for the historic preservation of monuments; art and sculpture projects in Berlin, Germany, and Europe. Projects in Russia (Moscow, St. Petersburg, Samara), Kazakhstan (Astana, Almaty, Aktau), Armenia, Azerbaijan, Georgia, Lithuania, Italy, and Austria.

Awards

2019	German Design Award 2020 Frankfurt/Main, Germany Project: Bolshevik factory courtyard, Moscow, Russia
2019	LUX life award, UK Best landscape architecture firm in 2019
2018	Russian National Landscape Architecture Award— Silver medal Category: best realized Residential Project— Project: Bolshevik factory, Moscow, Russia
2018	Echo Tech Green Award, Padua, Italy Project: United World College, together with Tim Flynn Architects, Dilijan, Armenia
2018	German Design Award, Frankfurt—Winner Project: Stone-Plant Sculpture, Dilijan, Armenia (Cat. 22, p. 74–75)
2017	A-Design Award, Como, Italy—Gold Award Project: History Park Moabit Prison, Berlin, Germany (Cat. 41, p. 118–125)
2017	A-Design Award, Como, Italy—Silver Award Project: Stone-Plant Sculpture, Dilijan, Armenia (Cat. 22, p. 74–75)
2017	City Brand and Landscape Award, Milan, Italy Special mention for Moabit City Garden in Berlin, Germany (Cat. 47 and 48, p. 140–145 are components of this project)
2017	International Garden Show IGA, Berlin Special mention for sustainable urban agriculture Project: Aquaponic Garden, IGA Berlin, Germany

2015	International Greenroof Leadership Award for Trendsetting Architecture Project: United World College in Dilijan, Armenia, together with Tim Flynn architects, London
2014	Russian National Landscape Architecture Award Silver medal for as yet unrealized social project on 2 hectares Project: Orangery, Gorki Park, Moscow, Russia
2007	German Landscape Architecture Prize, Federation of German Landscape Architects—First prize Project: History Park Moabit Prison, Berlin, Germany (Cat. 41, p. 118–125)
2007	Daylight Spaces Award—Danube University, Krems— First prize Project: History Park Moabit Prison, Berlin, Germany (Cat. 41, p. 118–125)
2007	Made in Germany—Best of Contemporary Architecture Staged by Brau Publishing House, Hamburg—Second prize Project: History Park Moabit Prison, Berlin, Germany (Cat. 41, p. 118–125)